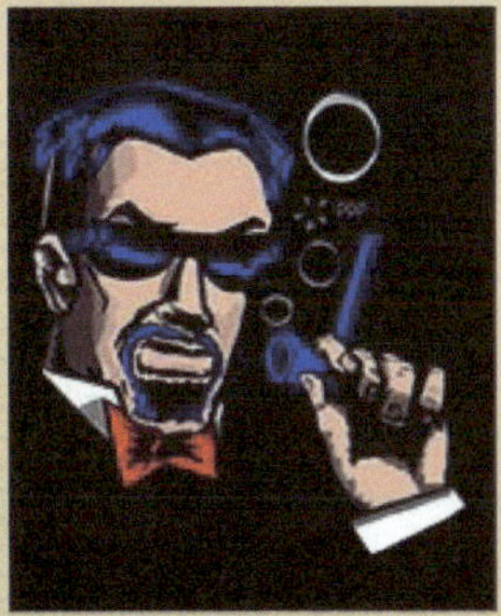

WELCOME TO "9 ARTS MAGAZINE"

'Ello, Ello 'Ello', Art Lovers (wherever yew are!)!! From border to border & all the ships at sea! (Cue Trumpets!) Roll up! Roll up &...

Country of first publication: United States of America & Canada

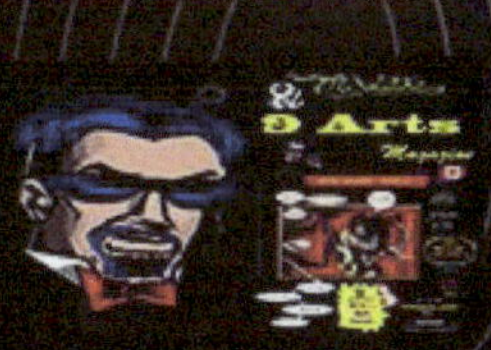

©MMXXI. by Mr. Watt c/o T.W. (International) Studios, c/o TonyWatt.com

For Ada, the Author's lovely late Mum!

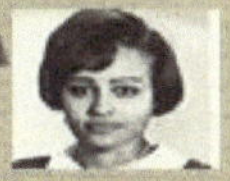

ISBN: 9798734489529

APRIL MMXXI ~ ISSUE #1

All of the 9 ARTS MAGAZINE publication's articles, graphics, artwork, storyboards, images, brands & logos are property of their respective owners.

Some of the documented opinions, humor &/or expressions in this informative arts & entertainment-based publication, are the individual speakers' own, and does not necessarily reflect the views of Mr. Watt, the 'zine's resident multi-media minded Author/Editor/Journo & Publisher; nor any of the other publication associated parties', as well. As well, Watt's revealing arts-articles, photos, BROTHER SOUL COMIX-related characters & the rest of his TWI Studio's creative properties, come from that tenacious P.T. Barnum-like mind! Said pop-culture hobbyist & (of recent) fine-arts enthusiast's new magazine series will focus on the intrntnl. arts scene & related pop-culture stuff-- showcasing the stunning works, as well as documenting the stories, methods influences that shaped the careers of these acclaimed (& also up-coming) talented artistes (who occupy one of, or a few positions in the 9 arts related mediums)! The author's own fictional works herein; are for entertainment purposes & not meant to offend. All rights reserved & protected under the copyright laws of Canada & the USA.

Unauthorized exhibition, distribution, or copying of this groovy arts magazine, or any part thereof, may result in civil action or, a snarky email. Any resemblance between the stick-figured 'toon characters (and the ballet dancer) in this publication and/or any persons, living, dead, or undead-- is a miracle! Some stories, names, characters, and incidents portrayed in this 9 ARTS MAGAZINE productions, that are fictitious-- have no identification with any actual people, places, buildings & products that is intended, or should be inferred. The author & his present artsy company within these pages, all hope you are well & diggin' in this page's BEV GRAPHIC shot, OVER the mother-lovin' Mr. Watt's snazzy lunch TABLE-MAT! That's *Info-tainment*, Folks!" And now--FROM **TonyWatt.com** comes: **9 ARTS MAGAZINE!** Please enjoy the ride! (Cue: Timpani!)

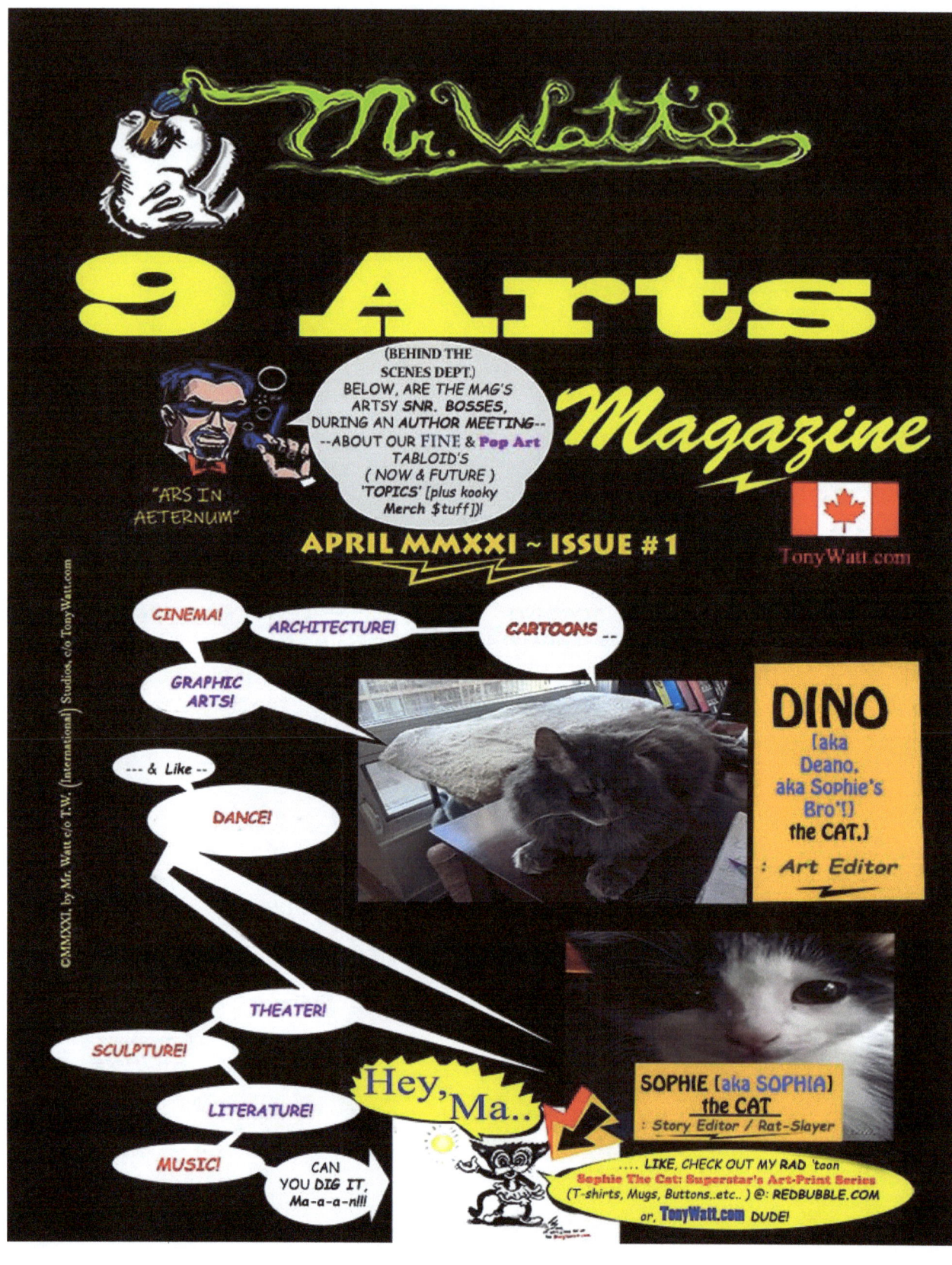

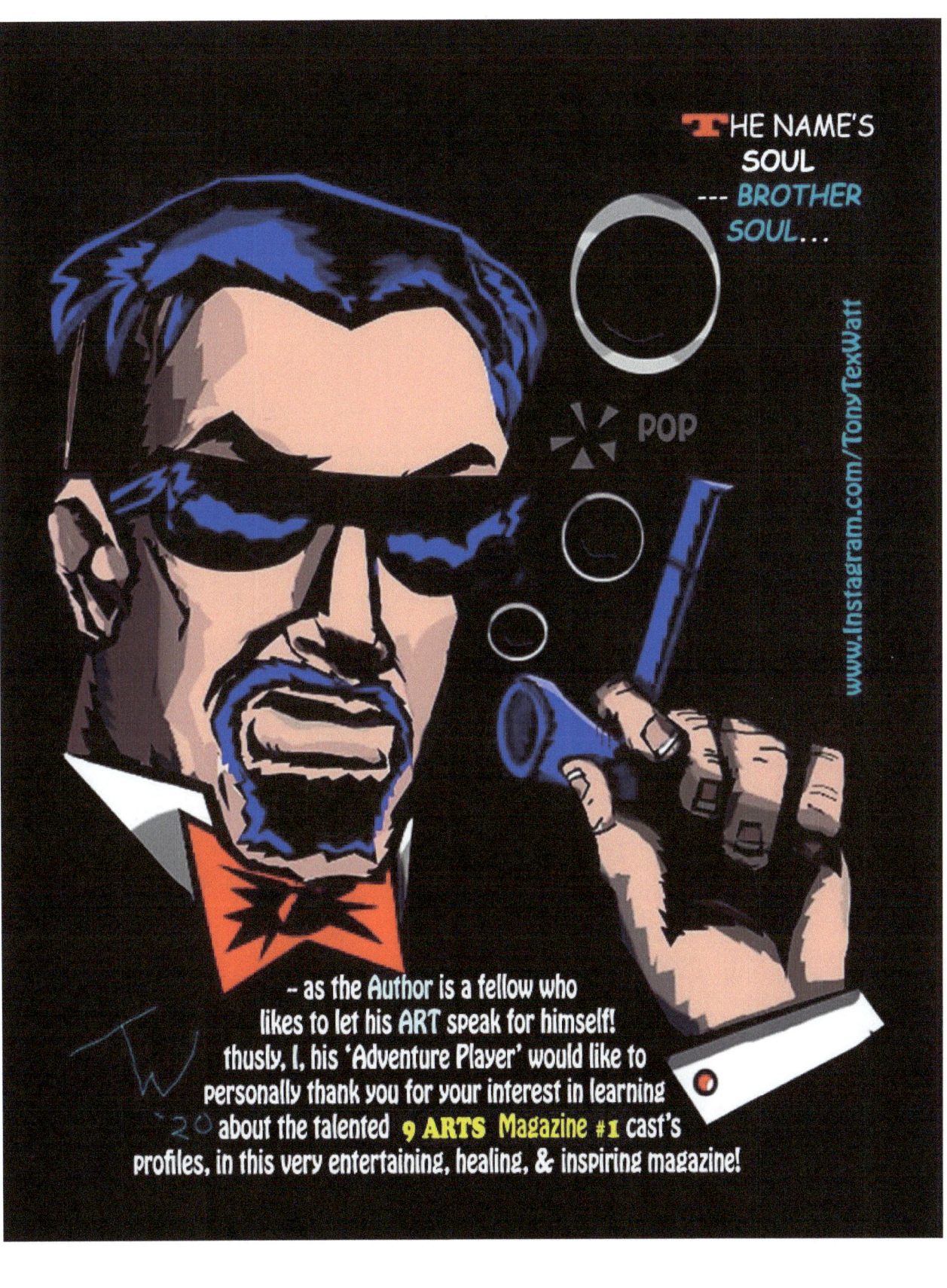

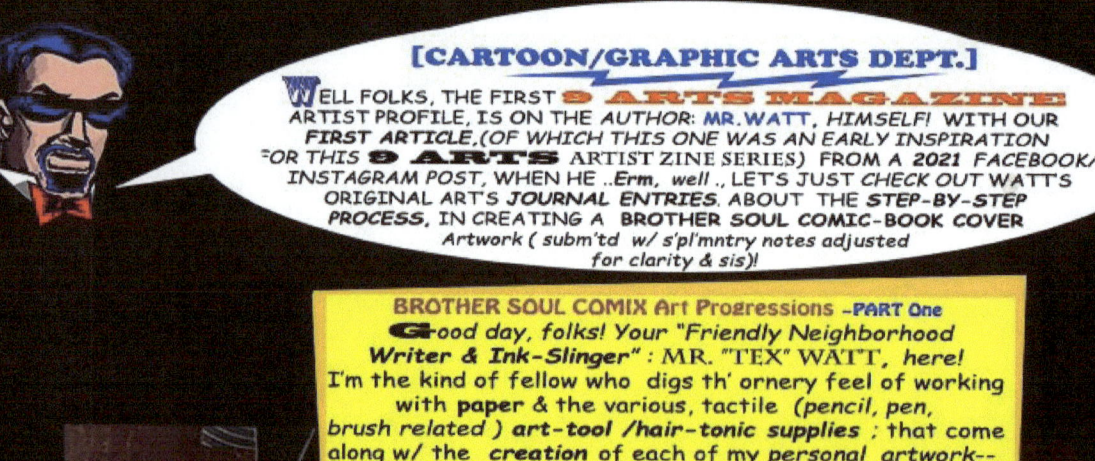

[CARTOON/GRAPHIC ARTS DEPT.]

Well folks, the first **9 ARTS MAGAZINE** artist profile, is on the author: **MR. WATT**, himself! With our *FIRST ARTICLE*, (of which this one was an early inspiration for this **9 ARTS** artist zine series) from a *2021* Facebook/Instagram post, when he ..Erm., well., let's just *CHECK OUT* Watt's original art's *JOURNAL ENTRIES*, about the *STEP-BY-STEP PROCESS*, in creating a BROTHER SOUL COMIC-BOOK COVER Artwork (subm'td w/ s'pl'mntry notes adjusted for clarity & sis)!

BROTHER SOUL COMIX Art Progressions - PART One

Good day, folks! Your *"Friendly Neighborhood Writer & Ink-Slinger"* : MR. "TEX" WATT, here! I'm the kind of fellow who digs th' ornery feel of working with **paper** & the various, tactile *(pencil, pen, brush related)* **art-tool /hair-tonic supplies** ; that come along w/ the **creation** of each of my personal **artwork**-- I'd like to avoid '**mechanical**' **artistic enhancement** as much as possible (that is except for **lettering**), in future.

The Loch Ness Pasta)

Mr. Tomato Head

Un-named (as yet) "Bird of Steel"

Jawbone Sam

By the way, this is *not an art-lesson*, but, a shared, artistic *Visual Art Journal*.

At any rate, I've decided today **[SAT./FEB./20/2021]**, to concentrate on going mostly **full-analog** with my **upcoming BROTHER SOUL COMIX** artwork (dispensing the practice of **digital computer coloring** -- which I've done in the past, on my original B&W [penciled & inked] fantasy/sci-fi adventure projects); seen in (independent) serial publications, such as this one for the **BROTHER SOUL COMIX SUPER-SPECIAL**.

I've included some of the BROTHER SOUL magazine's related **cartoon-based characters** above (in pencil) with their **names**, in case anyone wanted to read the **completed** published (& worded) **tracts**, in continuity, in said **picture-book series** [made under my **weirdo** horror host **pen-name:** KOUNT KRACULA])

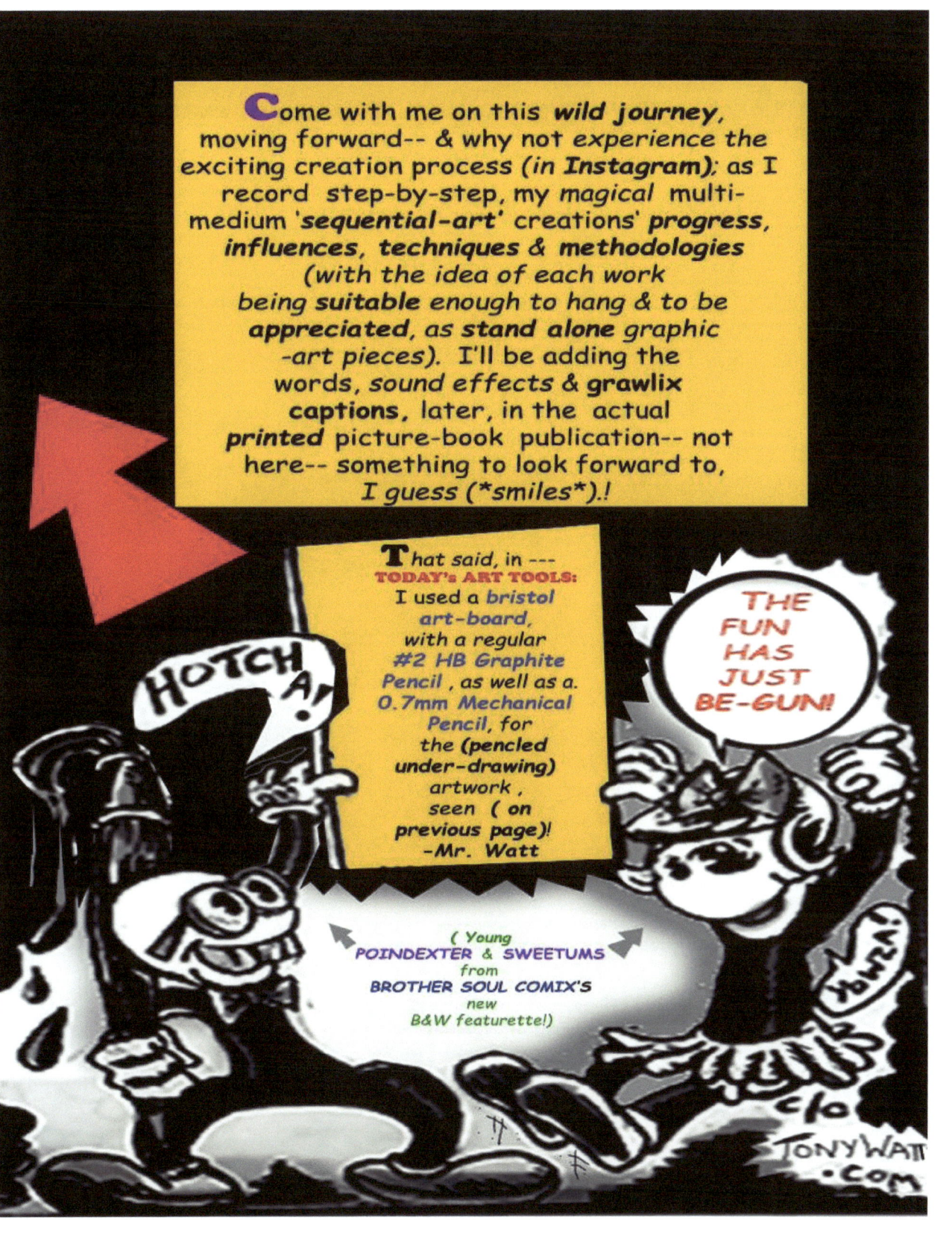

BROTHER SOUL COMIX Art Progressions — PART 02

As mentioned in my last blog--I like the *tactile* feel of the art tools & I certainly got my hands *dirty* today [Sun./FEB./21/2021], inking over the original pencils, on this BROTHER SOUL COMIX series' artwork, with (the Holy, **hirsute alien tomato-caveman** whackin'/**rabid monster-pasta** chokin' hero:) JAWBONE SAM!
And, [as of this writing] the *mysterious* metal duck, who seems to be making good on his *gambling bet!*

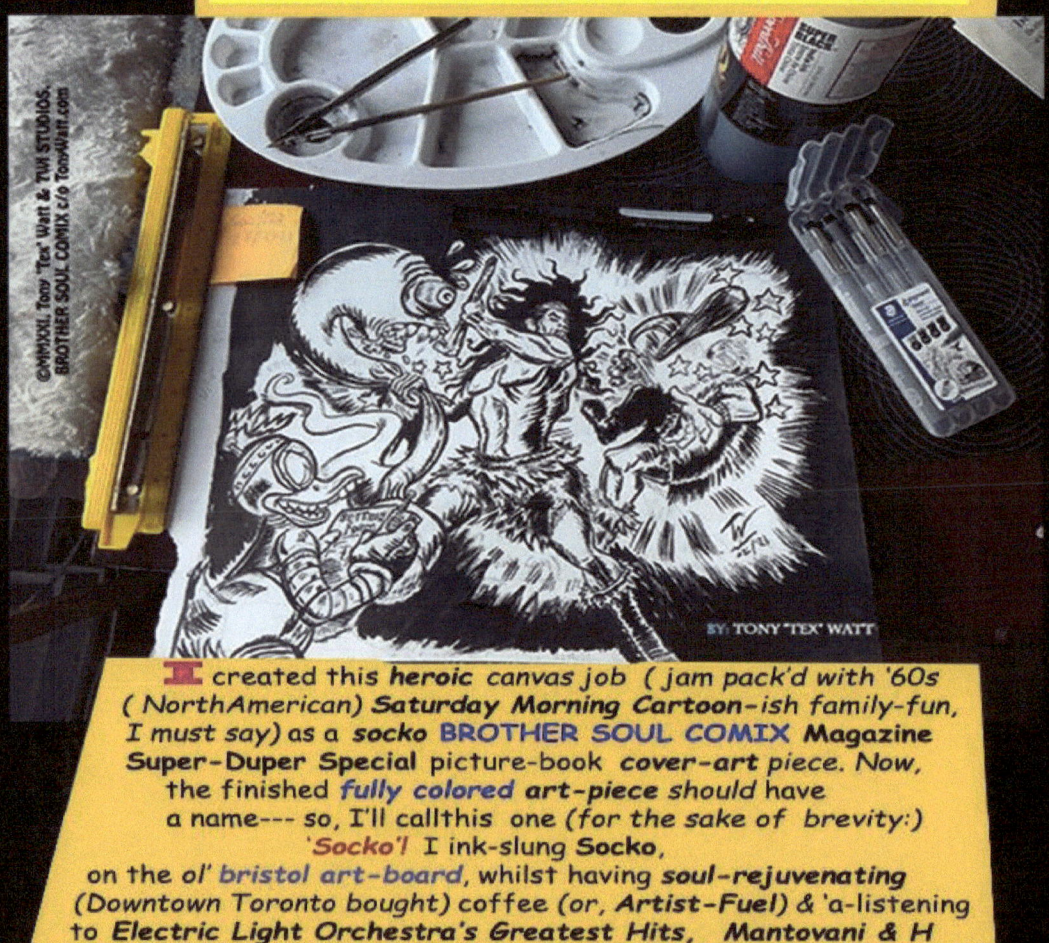

I created this *heroic canvas job* (jam pack'd with '60s (NorthAmerican) Saturday Morning Cartoon-ish family-fun, I must say) as a *socko* BROTHER SOUL COMIX Magazine Super-Duper Special picture-book cover-art piece. Now, the finished *fully colored* art-piece should have a name--- so, I'll call this one (for the sake of brevity:) 'Socko'! I ink-slung Socko, on the ol' *bristol art-board*, whilst having *soul-rejuvenating* (Downtown Toronto bought) coffee (or, Artist-Fuel) & 'a-listening to Electric Light Orchestra's Greatest Hits, Mantovani & H Henry Mancini (as well as vintage mid-20th Century, jazz, old country, roots reggae, classic rock & action-movie music sound-tracks), with my mixed cats (and story consultants) Sophia & Dino.

TODAY's ART TOOLS: I used regular SUPER-BLACK India Ink, various paint brushes, & a Faber-Castell XS artist pen (as well as as various sizes of *Steadler artist pens*), over the originally pencilled **under-drawing** layout).

BROTHER SOUL COMIX Art Progressions ~PART 03

I certainly enjoyed *breaking out* my old studio *coloring tools* today [*Mon./FEB./22/2021*] & working beside the blaring *phonograph stereo player* (as opposed to *clicking* in the picture's colors, on the studio P.C., in headphones). Personally, I think my new *artistic coloring* direction, seems more **vibrant** with the plethora of coloring *multi-mediums*, that I have at my disposal. I didn't realize that I had *so* many coloring implements to choose from (some, which I've had for *decades!*)-- I literally could *open up* an *art stationary* store! It's amazing how many related *art tools* we artists collect! *Wow!*

I get a great *kick* out of looking at this *canvas work*, for the (aforementioned) upcoming (as of this writing) **BROTHER SOUL COMIX Magazine Super-Duper Special** picture-book cover-art (but then, I'm *biased*..ha ha!).

Although I've not 100% completed this **'Socko'** piece, so far--

-- I'm growing weary & will turn in early tonite, AFTER digitally lettering this artist log --

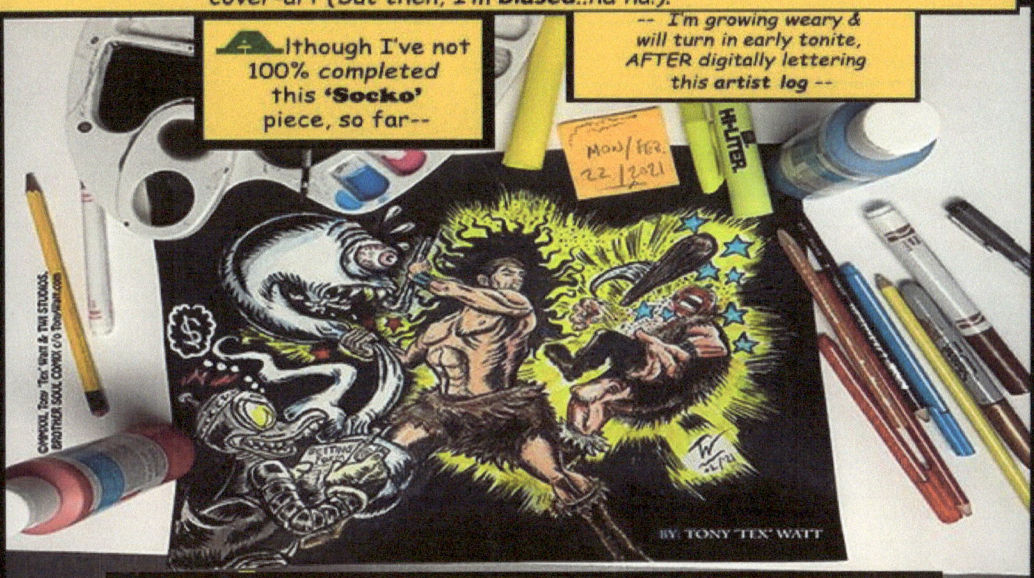

I'm also happy to say that I had a real *blast* making this initial *nouveau-designed* work [whilst listening to the Beatles' **White Album** & also, Ella Fitzgerald & Louis Armstrong's **'Ella And Louis'** LP] & I look forward to *documenting* even more of my *upcoming artwork*, in a similar manner, for sure!

It also helps that I enjoy drawing these kooky self-created comic-book adventure characters, from my published cartoon world (that I call: the 'Chuckle-verse')!
~TODAY's ART TOOLS: For coloring, I used watered-down SUPER-BLACK India Ink, various markers / pencil crayons, Hi-liters & acrylic paint, over the originally inked bristol art-board layout. c/o **TonyWatt.com**

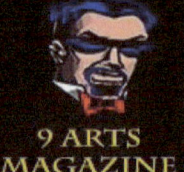

9 ARTS MAGAZINE

[CINEMA Dept.]

TROMA ENTERTAINMENT FILMMAKER: LLOYD KAUFMAN'S
"TROMEO & JULIET"
A 24th ANNIVERSARY RETROSPECTIVE

By: Mr. Watt

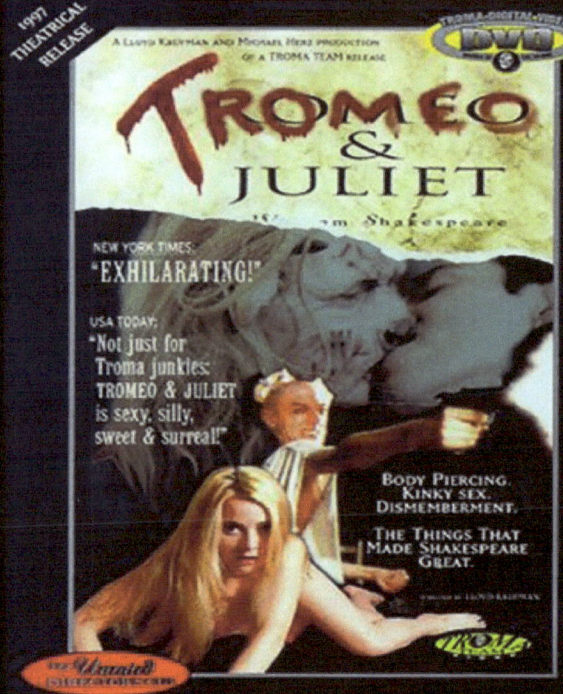
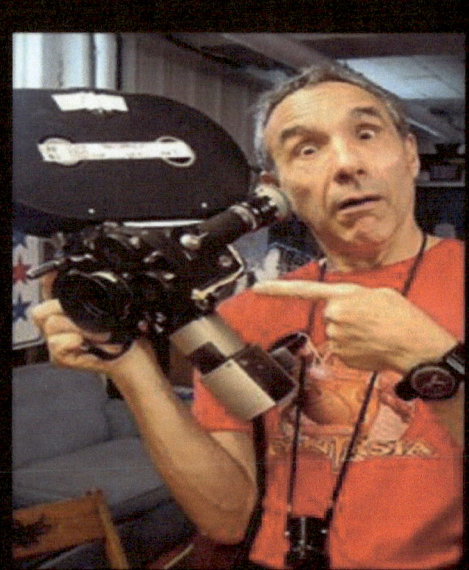

"*Lloyd's* body of work has now proven to be a seminal influence on film today. Just look at any film created by the likes of Quentin Tarantino, Takashi Miike, Peter Jackson, Eli Roth, Gasper Noe, or James Gunn, to name a few, and you are likely watching a film influenced by *Class of Nuke 'Em High, Tromeo & Juliet,* or *Citizen Toxie.*"
-Stan Lee (Comic-book Icon)

TROMEO & JULIET (1997) gives the maverick finger to cinematic subtly. The film was made by the notorious, iconoclastic self made legend & outspoken Godfather of 21st Century Independent Cinema : Lloyd Stanley Kaufman Jr. (born : New York City, New York, December 30, 1945; to Ruth (née Fried) and lawyer Stanley Lloyd Kaufman, Sr.).

Filmmaker **Lloyd Kaufman** with his mutant cinematic creation **The Toxic Avenger**, or **"Toxie"** Troma Entertainment's official mascot!

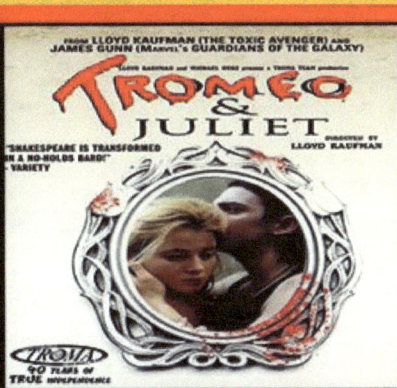

"(TROMEO & JULIET) ..Has poetry to match its sex and gore."
– The New York Times

Kaufman is an influential & popular U.S.A. based independent director, producer, writer, actor who has helped to shape the landscape of today's mainstream 'frat boy' cinema (and one that introduced many modern stars from **Trey Parker**, to **Samuel L. Jackson**). Many low-brow comedies today, from **The Hangover (2009)** to **Superbad (2007)**, to the **Scary Movie** comedy franchise-- owes heavily to the cinematic stylings of Kaufman's influential and notoriously wacky Troma Entertainment film studio.

In the late 1960's, Kaufman was enrolled at Yale University (where he would later give his famous "Make Your Own Damn Movie" Master Class), diligently working on a respectable degree in Chinese Studies.

However, Kaufman was destined for other things. As he explains in his hit book 'All I Need To Know About Filmmaking I Learned From The Toxic Avenger', (published by Penguin Putnam), At Yale I was placed in a dormitory room with two film fanatics, and I knew everything had irrevocably changed."

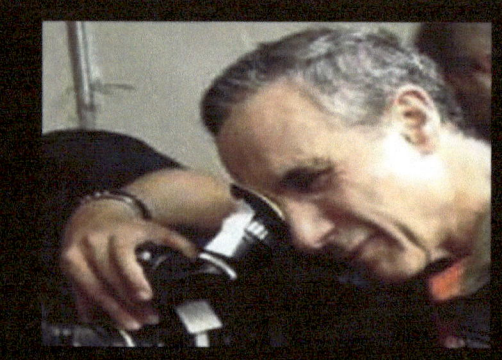

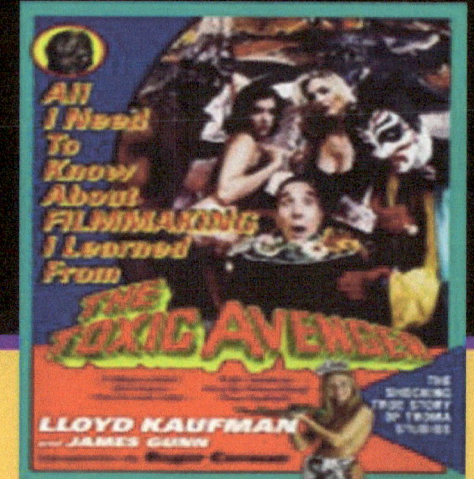

In fact, Kaufman was infected with a love of movies, from which he never recovered.

In 1971, Kaufman met his future Troma Entertainement partner Michael Herz, at Yale.

The Troma Universe was born in 1974, with a series of highly original, raunchy comedies such as Squeeze Play! (1979), Stuck On You! (1982), Waitress! (1981), and other titles ending with an exclamation point!

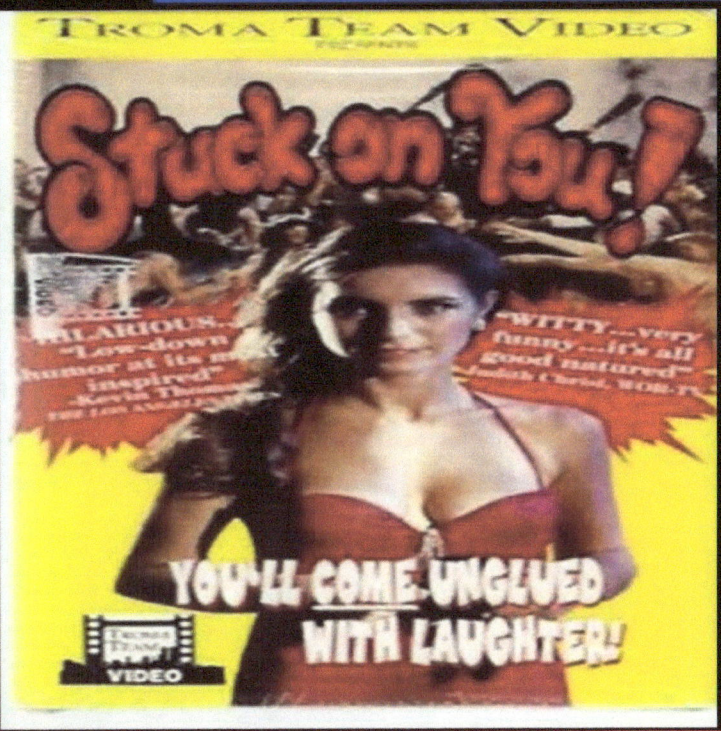

Kaufman has stated that Stuck on You! is his favorites of Troma's "sexy comedies."

These movies were independent precursors to such later smash genre hits as National Lampoon's Animal House (1978) and Porky's (1982). Though these new T&A flicks movies did well financially-- Kaufman still continued to work on such outside film productions; such as Rocky (1976) and Saturday Night Fever (1977). But, Kaufman's relationship with mainstream Hollywood would not last long. "There were problems," Kaufman said, "as I always wanted to do things my own way and my employers insisted I do things the correct way."

Lloyd continued to build up a list of impressive credits------ as well as some overpowering debts, to pawnbrokers nationwide. Kaufman proved his former Hollywood employers wrong, with his breakthrough movie, The Toxic Avenger (1984)!

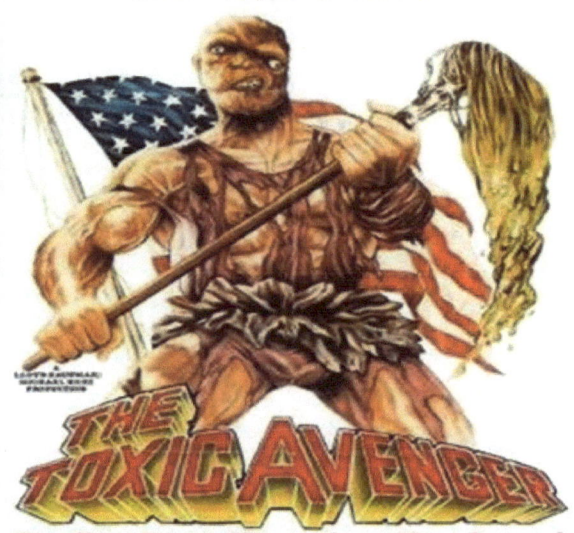

" ---maniacally farcical sense of humor."

- The New York Times (1986)

This tale of a health club mop-boy named Melvin (played by Mitchell Cohen) who is transformed into a hideously deformed creature of superhuman size and strength, struck a chord with audiences and critics alike! The maverick Kaufman & Herz's independent Troma Studios demonstrated that there were a large number of people who were interested in seeing things done Kaufman's way-- and a film series was born.

The Toxic Avenger film, soon led to the creation of a popular animated television series: "Toxic Crusaders ('91)," which spawned several different related cartoon book titles, published by Marvel (& most recently, Troma's own independent comic book imprint) and three other feature-film sequels. The most recent title, in the series is Citizen Toxie: The Toxic Avenger Part IV (2000)!

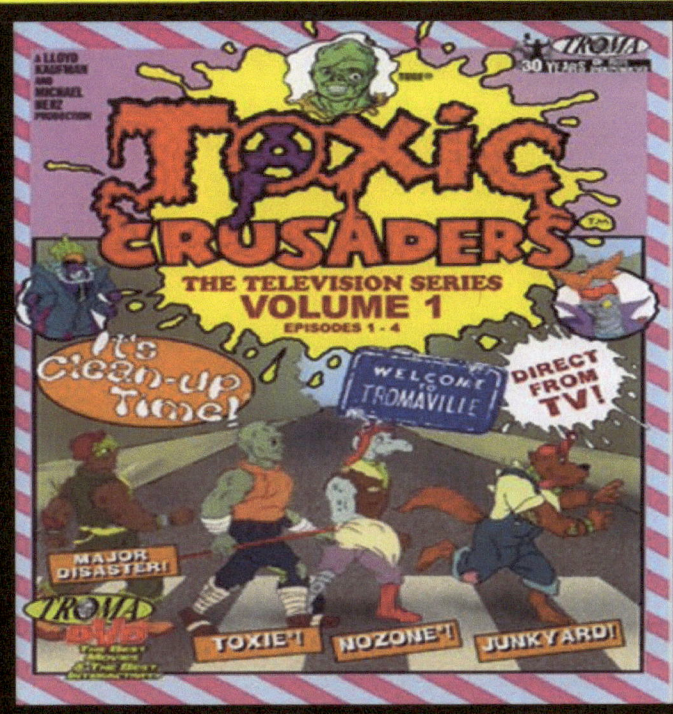

The success of The Toxic Avenger was followed by a string of commercial and artistic triumphs in a similar vein--- blending fantasy, heavy action, comedy and eroticism-- in a style that can only be described as "Tromatic".

These films, including the *Class of Nuke 'Em High* series, *Sgt. Kabukiman NYPD (1990)* and *Troma's War (1988)*, were often ignored or scorned by the mainstream intelligentsia of the time but spoke to an entire generation of young people who rejected the pandering, commercial films of the mid-to-late 1980's. Some of these Troma fans went on to become filmmakers themselves, including Quentin Tarantino, James Gunn, Kevin Smith, Mike Judge, Peter Jackson, and Trey Parker!

"As an inexpensive exploitation film, "Class of Nuke 'Em High" has its moments of ---maniacally redeeming lunacy."

- The New York Times (1986)

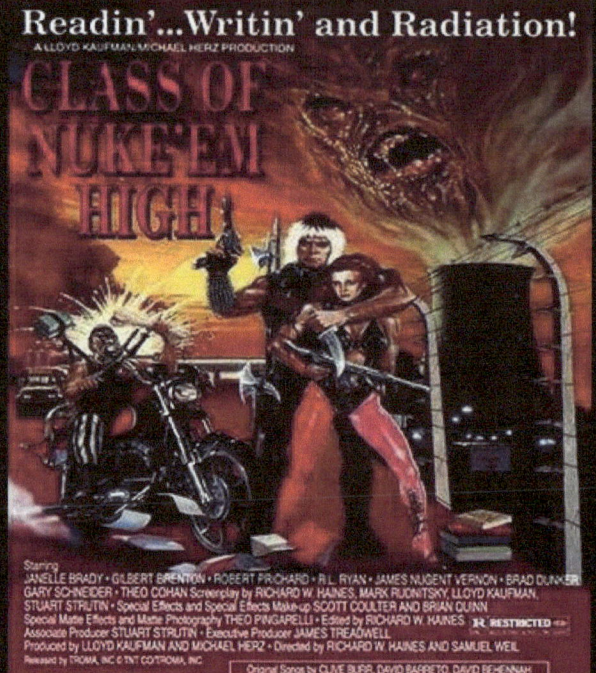

Thanks to these admirers, Kaufman has been asked to make cameo appearances in films like Trey Parker's *Orgazmo (1997)*, Eli Roth's *Cabin Fever (2007)* & James Gunn's *Guardians of the Galaxy (2014)*. In the nineties, Kaufman and the Troma Team began to win respect from even their harshest critics. In '97, the *Tromeo & Juliet* comedy feature became a surprise theatrical and critical hit. This progressive, colorful movie is on of my favorite comedies in my personal DVD collection (under the 'Bizarro' category. Lloyd Kaufman has always claimed that he was creating cinematic 'Art', as he mentions in another of my favorite Troma movies-- the self-referential 1999 horror/comedy: *Terror Firmer* (loosely based on his filmmaking book series-- & also one of the seminal inspirations for my own original descent into 'outsider' B-movie making 'madness').

The TROMEO & JULIET movie, flips the bird to the time's mainstream romantic movies... It was new, lewd, cartoonish, violent, gory and comedy-sexually over the top (one critic even called the movie "gloriously f*cked up")! Tromeo & Juliet, is the first 20th Century movie I'd ever seen, that foreshadowed the darker, uncompromising spirit and plucky youth-quake renaissance of the turn of this past century.

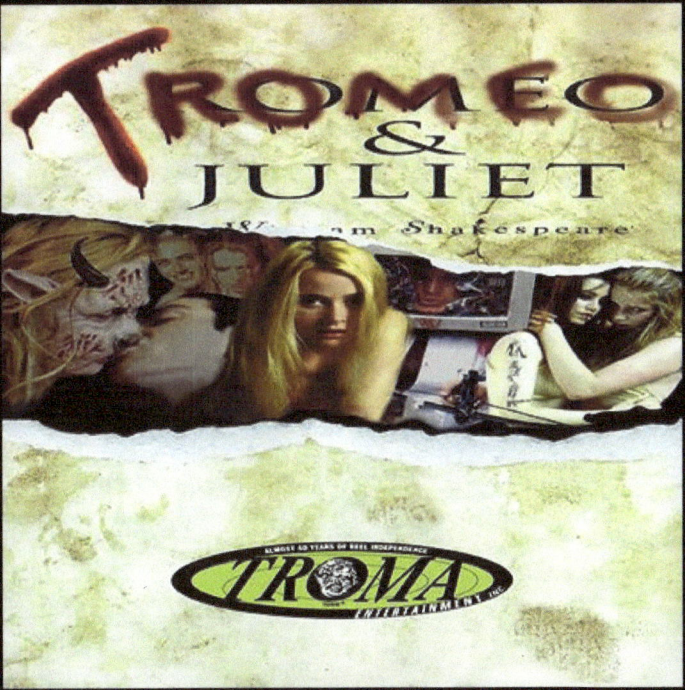

"Tromeo and Juliet, directed by Lloyd Kaufman from a screenplay he wrote with James Gunn, is to Hollywood B-movies what Mad magazine is to comic books."

- The New York Times (1997)

Indeed, I believe Troma Entertainment (and Tromeo & Juliet, in particular) was again, ahead of its time, in capturing the philistine spirited, apathetic malaise of what was to the early 2000's nihilistic 'college-humored' motion pictures, satires; such as the American Pie series (as much as the Troma influenced "Porky's" & Co. was, to '80s low-brow films & Kirby/Lee's Marvel Comic's & D.C.'s effect on 'superhero' comic-books, in the 1960s & '70s). Though my personal retro-artistic & entertainment tastes have evolved & mellowed over time-- thankfully, for the dissident B-MOVIE lover---Troma Entertainment & Kaufman has not. But, as a young, excitable hipster 'Candide' -like (thx. for the recommend, Mr. K.)youth of the 90's-- to me, Tromeo & Juliet was very subversively appealing! I'd naively thought this movie was the bom'diggity!

TROMEO & JULIET is a satirical dark-comedy, jam packed, with crazy, kinetic, hyperactive, violent morally & slapstic-burlesque/sexually subversive N.Y. vs euro-filmic characters. There are many scenes of comedic perversion, fantasy, surrealism, fetishism, satire & cartoon violence.

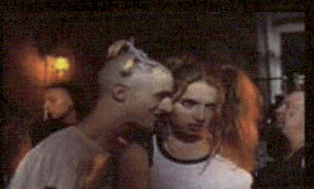

"Jensen (Juliet) brings moments of affecting, wide-eyed tenderness to her assignment, and does she ever look out of place." -San Francisco Examiner

"Shakespeare is transformed in a no-holds Bard!"
– Variety

"Not Just For Troma Junkies: Tromeo & Juliet is Sexy, Silly, Sweet and Surreal!"
– USA Today

" ...it's crude, it's crass - and it's pretty damn funny...
...the two leads, Will Keenan (Tromeo) and Jane Jensen (Juliet), exude believeable chemistry.."
-Efilmcritic.com (2003)

The movie, is of it's time: with many of it's players reflecting the grittier, existentialist, apathetic and 'extre-e-me' (to use a popular '90s term) attitudes of angry '90s' post-modern North American youth culture & the early 2000's 'frat-boy' comedy movies, for the MTV weaned, attention deficit, 'live for today' Generation Y-- who grew up learning to 'Just say no!' & watching safe, boring t.v. programs, like 'The Cosby Show' & where tired of the sanctimonious cultural mediocrity, of the hyper-commercialized mainstream-fed media.
Though my personal artistic & entertainment tastes has changed & mellowed over time-- thankfully, for the dissident B-movie enthusiast-- Lloyd Kaufman & Troma Entertainment has not. But, as a young, excitable jazz-hepster'd, ponytailed, youth in the 90's-- to me --Tromeo & Juliet had a very cool & subversive cult appeal. I had never seen such filmic nihilism and was hungry for the stuff! I thought this movie was the bomb! I still find it highly entertaining, over beer!

The movie's rebelious, gross-out appeal is not for everyone, I must say honestly- But, for those of us youngsters in the 1990s, who felt disenfranchised by the bourgeoisie (& were sold a bag of hypocritical goods, from the now material-minded, middle-class, ex-hippie generation) ---it was!

That said Tromeo & Juliet is still to his day, a funny & dead-on satirical (if not, artistically anomalous) film. And, the two lead actors that play the star crossed lovers; handle their roles charmingly well-- with passionate retro-romantic innocence; mixed with the movie's hard rocking, post-boomer decadent spirit. T&J was selected for screening at the Italian Fantafestival, where it won the award for Best Film of 1997.

"..viewers with the stomach to endure the unsavoury elements may find that Kaufman's work contributes to discourse surrounding Romeo and Juliet, in some surprisingly nuanced ways." - Writus Andronicus Blog

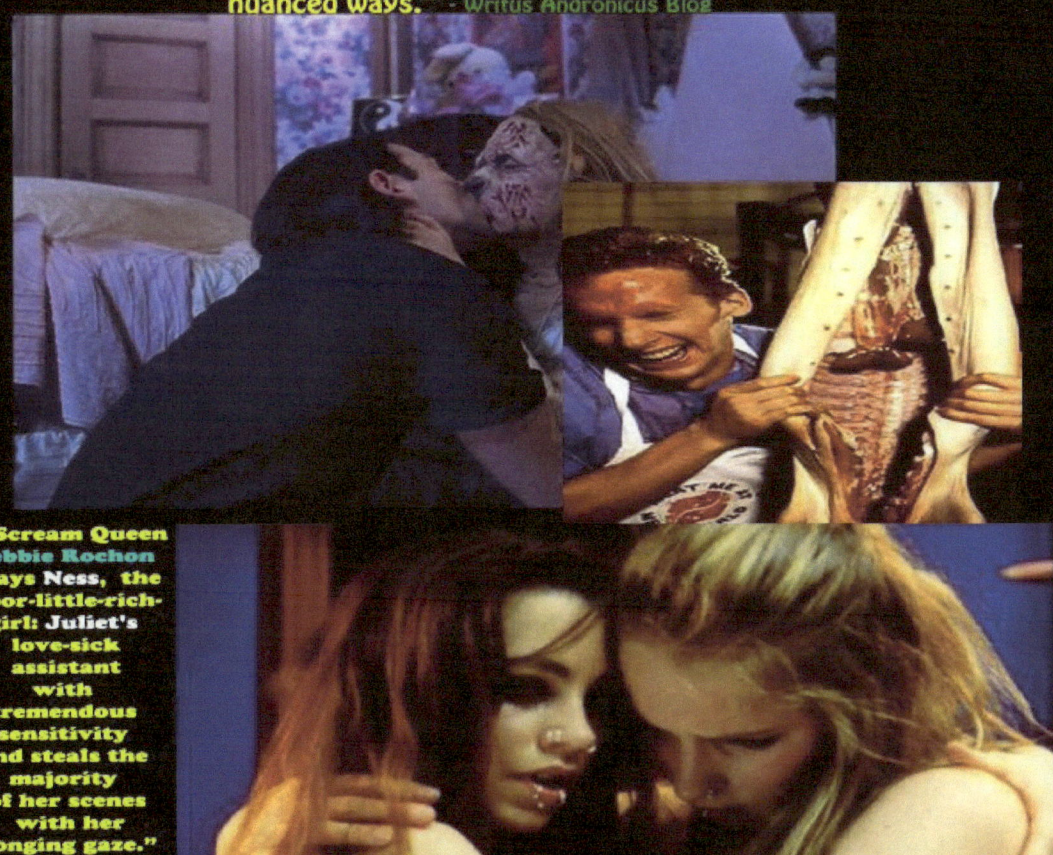

" Scream Queen Debbie Rochon plays Ness, the poor-little-rich-girl: Juliet's love-sick assistant with tremendous sensitivity and steals the majority of her scenes with her longing gaze."
-HorrorDNA.com

Scream starlet: Debbie Rochon (above, w/ Juliet actress Jensen) burns up the screen with a deviant, erotic, sexually charged performance, as NESS, the facial ring ladened Capulet family family servant, in one of her best film roles.

The main movie plot (that is also failed to be mentioned, says Kaufman, in the original 1597 Shakespeare Romeo & Juliet play:), is about two warring clans .. renamed, retold & performed in a pseudo-Shakespearean style, in a modern-day ['90s] Manhattan setting), is about a the poor Tromeo Que, a young man who lives in a squalor (with his alcoholic father, Monty) & spends much of his days on his home personal computer screen watching CD-ROM pornography. Tromeo then eventually falls in love with a young mansion dwelling, sexually confused and very much harrassed young lady.named Julie Capulet, who's demented father runs a porn empire. Julie is also protected by her overbearing cousin: Tyrone..one of the more memorable male charcters in the movie.

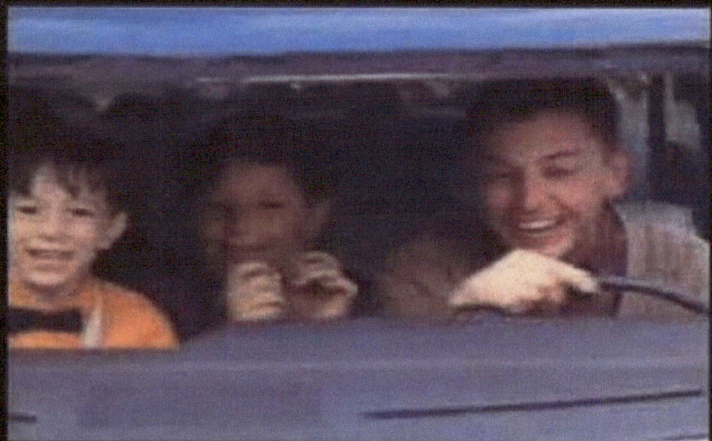

One of my favorite T&J comedic stand-outs, is a charming throw-back slapstick gag, involving a typical nuclear yuppie family in a car, gleefully singing "Found a Peanut," and stock stuntwork footage (I won't spoil the scene here-- but, it's a must see)!

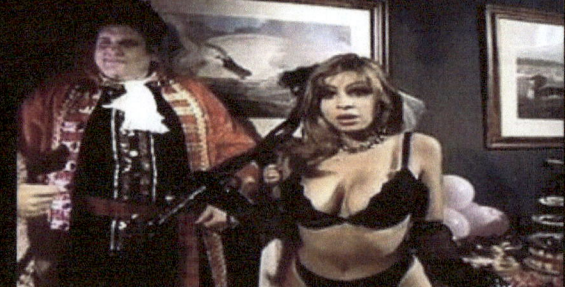

Actress & Marvel Comics' 'Nightcat' comic-book inspiration: Jacqueline Tavarez (in the above pix, in black lingerie) burns up the screen, with her campy role, in T&J, as a cartoonishly, burlesque nymphomaniac, named "Rosy"; who dates Tromeo (Keenan) and invariably cheats on him, every moment she gets.

Amongst the usual Troma movie mayhem; T&J also shows an actual, dance hall humor & graphic piercing mix (which foreshadows the early 21st Century's popular, youthful obsession with body piercing.. like Ness)...which I've never fully understood, myself (--- but then, I'm old).

During a retrospective on Troma, done by a British Film Festival", Kaufman declared, "I visited Shakespeare's birthplace in Stratford-Upon-Avon. Whilst there, Shakespeare's spirit entered my body. I cannot reveal from which orifice Shakespeare's spirit exited my body, but it wasn't long after that; that Tromeo & Juliet was delivered to the world." Upon elaborating in his memoirs, 'All I Need to Know About Filmmaking I Learned from the Toxic Avenger', Kaufman wrote that the concept for the Tromeo & Juliet feature came to him in a "visionary burst" and stemmed from a "desire to do romance", not to mention the urge to use the title, which he found humorous.

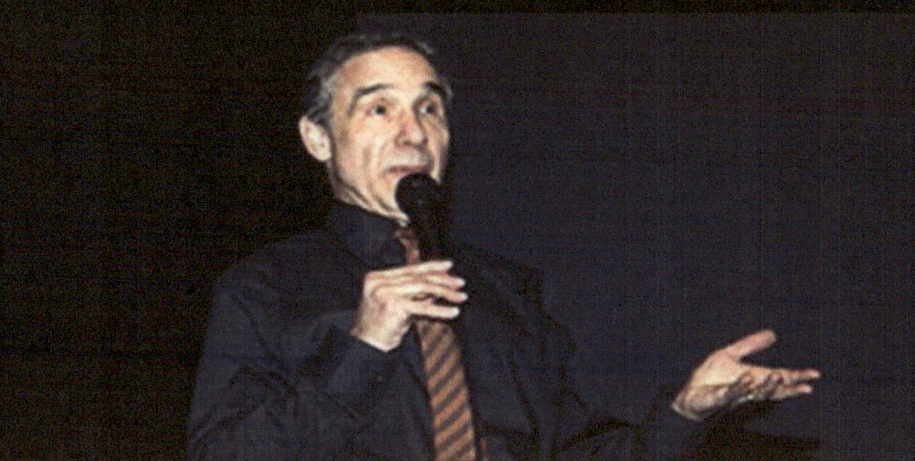

After completing several drafts of the script, Jill Champtaloup, a lady friend of Mr. Kaufman's at HBO/Cinemax forwarded him the resume of a student enrolled in the Columbia University Masters Program who might help complete the screenplay. His name was James Gunn and she had written: "He's your man", on the resume... just like an Ol' Westerner.

Something else on Gunn's resume popped out at Kaufman: it was an attached article from The St. Louis Post Dispatch, about Gunn's career as a performance artist. The article claimed that Gunn had vomited onstage. Whether it was from nervousness or for entertainment value or a critical assessment of Terrence Malick's career, it didn't really say – but still! A publicly vomiting writer, appealed to the out-of-the box thinking Kaufman! "I felt like Zero Mostel in the (movie) The Producers (1968) when he saw Dick Shawn audition...", Lloyd later wrote, "I was pretty sure that James Gunn was ours."!

Kaufman and Gunn soon went to work, bouncing ideas off one another & working out the kinks in the story, creating what Kaufman described as 'Troma's best script.' "It's funny!," Kaufman told Gunn upon completing the script and reflecting on the changes they had made to the Bard's tragedy. "You're at the beginning of your career with nothing to lose, so you're going all the way with this thing, making it as extreme as possible.'

Lloyd continued, "I felt like I'm at the point in my career when I have everything to lose, so I'm going all the way with it. Somehow we're at two utterly different points in our lives but in the same exact place.".

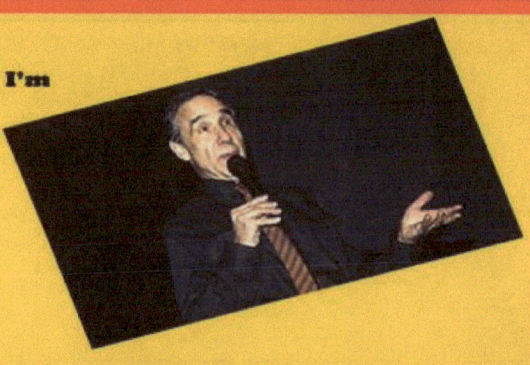

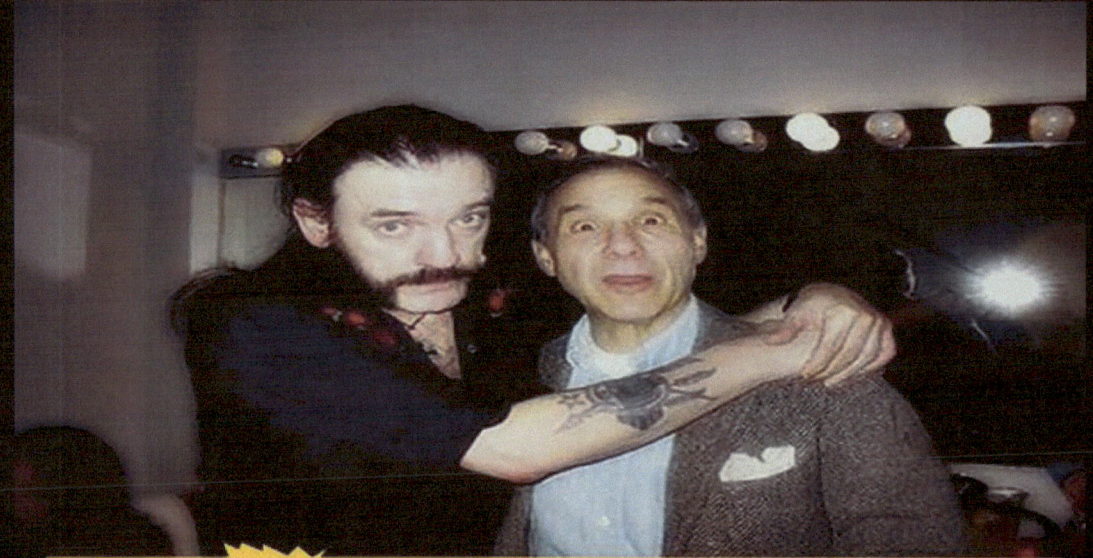

Upon its release, complete with a (heavy metal rock band :) 'Motorhead' soundtrack (featuring the late Lemmy Kilmister, seen in above pix with Lloyd) and the tag-line; "Body Piercing. Kinky Sex. Dismemberment. "The Things That Made Shakespeare Great!" Tromeo & Juliet played in theaters around the world. It broke house attendance records in Seattle and San Francisco and played for almost a year in Los Angeles.

Still, Tromeo & Juliet received high praise from the mainstream media:
"Exhilarating!" - The New York Times
"Hilarious!" - LA Times
"A Winner!" - New York Post
"Sexy, Silly, Sweet & Surreal!" - USA Today
"Totally Over-The-Top!" - Saint Louis Post Dispatch
"Outrageously Funny!" - London Daily Mail

Tromeo & Juliet celebrated T&J's 15th year anniversary, with a 2012 screening at the New Beverly Cinema in Los Angeles, hosted by Lloyd Kaufman and James Gunn.

The film is beloved by many fans and has enjoyed continued success on home video---
---having been released on Troma VHS, Laserdisc, DVD, Blu-ray & , most recently, Video-on-Demand. Actor: Kenneth Branagh and 'Crash' novelist J.G. Ballard both were knocked out by Tromeo & Juliet, at the Cannes Film Festival, according to Kaufman.

Shortly thereafter, Romeo and Juliet (1996), by Baz Luhrmann and some obscure actors named DeCaprio and Claire Danes came out and, was a smash hit.

Said film's glory gave further extended box office life to Tromeo & Juliet.

Kaufman's next directed opus:
Terror Firmer (1999)
--- inspired by the book:
'All I Need To Know About Filmmaking I Learned From The Toxic Avenger'---

----played for six months in Los Angeles alone.

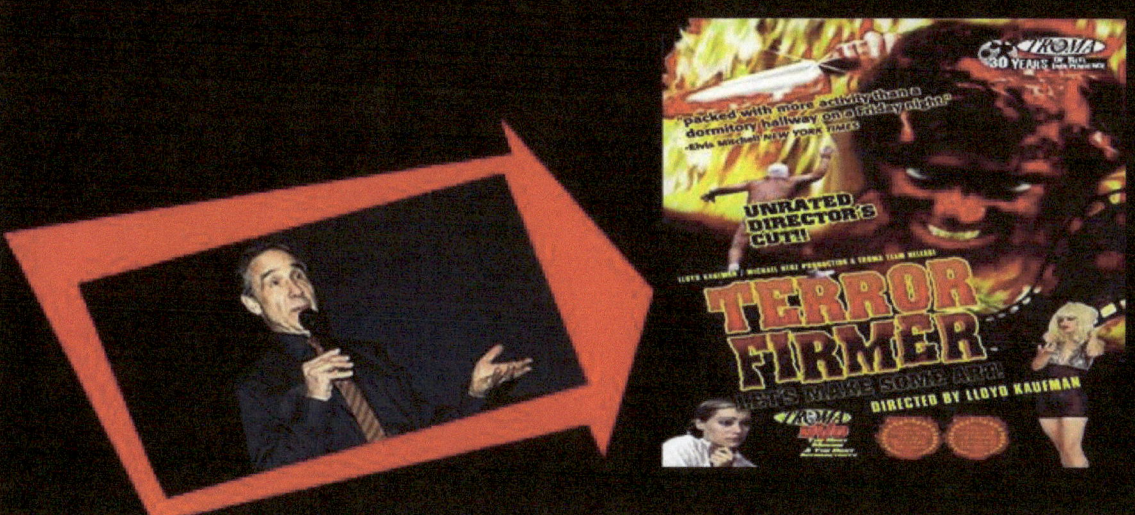

In addition, **Kaufman** has been an *honored guest* at various international film festivals and , *Troma retrospectives* around the world. **The San Sebastian Film Festival, the British Film Institute, the Cinematheque Francaise, the American Cinematheque, the Chicago International Film Festival, the UCLA Film Archives, the Tokyo Film Festival & the Shanghai International Film Festival** ---are just a few of the venues to have showered Kaufman with praise and *free booze!*

Kaufman has received multi-**Lifetime Achievement Awards**, at events like *the Fantasy Film Festival of Amsterdam, Sitges Film Festival, Brussels Festival of Fantasy* & others.

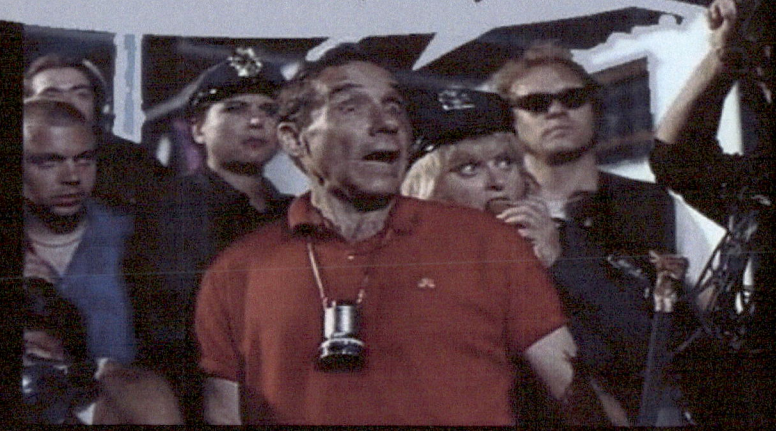

On **January 1999**, Kaufman founded the **TromaDance Film Festival** in Park City, Utah. Determined to give *independent film* back to the people, Kaufman established a *festival* where there is no *entry fee*, for **filmmakers** to submit their *films*, nor is there any admission charged to truly valued audience members..

The TromaDance Film Festival presents a broad spectrum of **films** and **film styles**, creating an opportunity for everyone to put their own personal vision on film and have it seen. Kaufman is also a *tireless innovator*, constantly using new **developments in technology** to foster the growth of *independent art*. Troma Ent'mnt. has a dynamic web presence with *Troma.com*, *TromaDance.com*, *PoultrygeistMovie.com* & the VOD streaming service *(Troma Now)* @ watch.troma.com

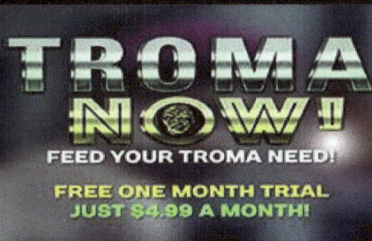

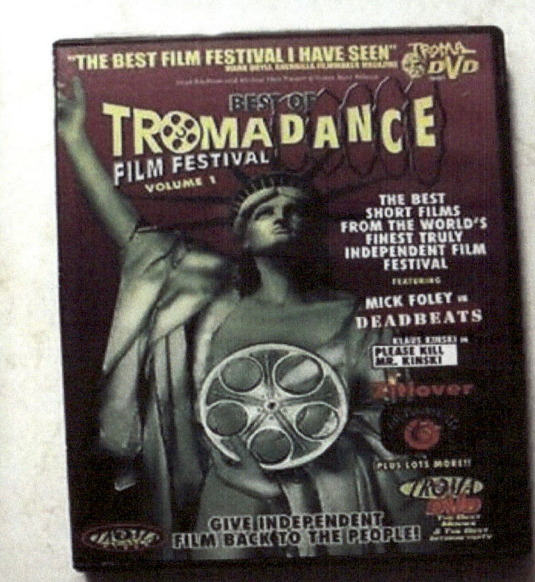

The personable *Mr. Lloyd Kaufman's* loyal worldwide fans also created the fan site **LloydKaufman.com** **T**roma has also been ahead of the curve in *DVD production*-- releasing *feature-packed titles* since 1997. Kaufman has also earned the **respect & trust** of his peers in the indie filmmaking community; serving *two terms (2007-2011)* as the elected *Chairman of the Independent Film & Television Alliance*, composed of 200 **member companies**.

As of this writing, The Toxic Avenger is slated to undergo a Hollywood remake, starring Peter Dinklage (Game of Thrones).

Kaufman and Troma co-Founder, Michael Herz's most recent co-productions are the critically acclaimed Father's Day (2011), **RETURN TO NUKE 'EM HIGH** VOLS. 1 & 2 (2013 & '17 -- both Return to Nuke 'Em High movies [sequels to Class of Nuke 'Em High] are, as Kaufman says, are I.. satirical sci-fi comedies), with themes ...ripped straight from today's headlines----, and love triumphing over prejudice...I

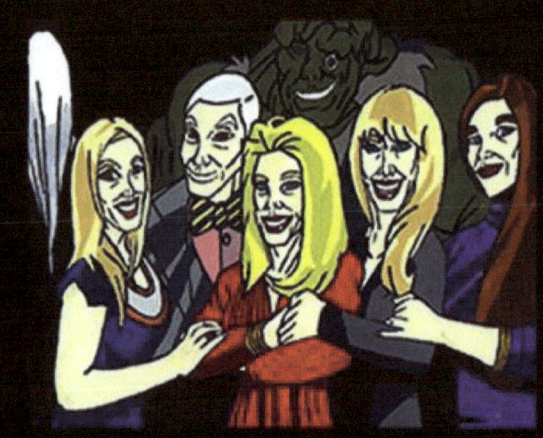

On the personal front, Lloyd has three daughters – Lily Hayes, Lisbeth and Charlotte. He served on the Board of Directors at Trinity School in New York City. His beloved wife of 48 years , Patricia, is the N. Y. State Film Commissioner..

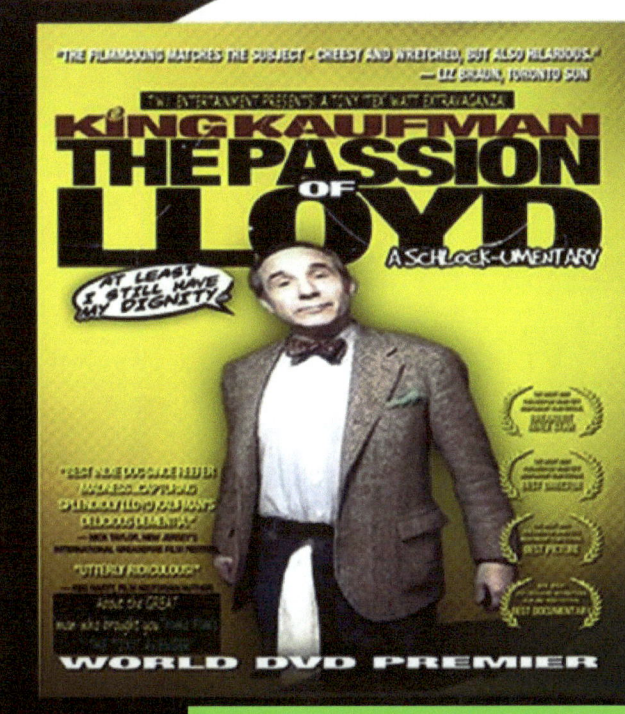

Troma's slogan in 2014 was *"40 years of Disrupting Media"*. Another slogan Kaufman & the company has used, is *"Movies of the Future!"* During film-studies-- I first saw **Tromeo and Juliet'** on VHS, in 2000,; as (as a young, *naive*, *idiot* brit-rock 'hepster' /*metal-hea*d) ---on a java *trip*.. I told **Lloyd**, years later (when he was the subject of **King Kaufman: The Passion of Lloyd [2008]** a famous **UNKNOWN** (indie) doco; I produced),- --- later watching **T&J** again, sober- realizing that I didn't need the hot drink's *buzz*...

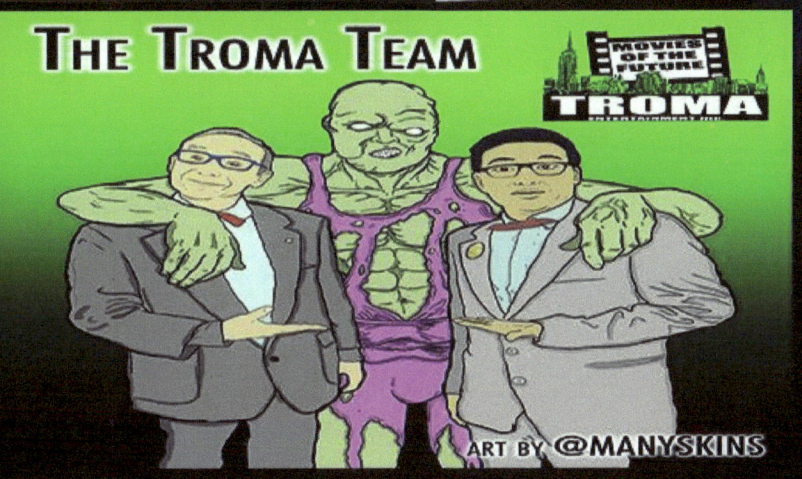

According to Wikipedia, **Troma** has produced, acquired and distributed **over 1,000 independent films** since its creation. To his & Mr. Toxie's many rabid 'outsider' movie fans... **Lloyd Stanley Kaufman Jr.** is truly a self-made legend (a quick thank you to **Thom DeMicco** [Assistant to Lloyd Kaufman], for your valued story assistance)!

~Mr. Watt, Mar./ 22/ 2021

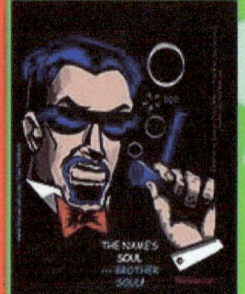

Next is a **Q&A** that the mag's author did, with (the always *eccentrically* mirthful &) *ever-quotable* Mr. *Lloyd Kaufman*. Enjoy, folks! -Ol' Bro' So'l!

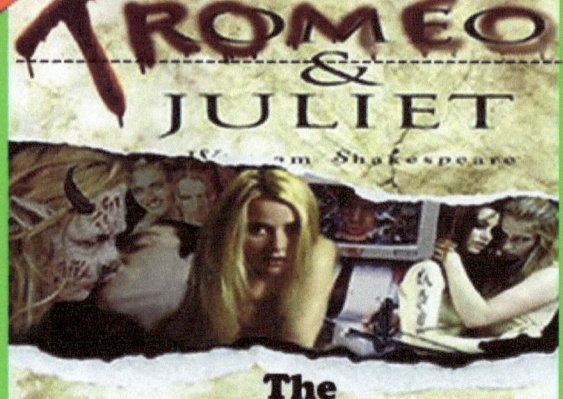

The **LLOYD KAUFMAN/ TROMA** Tromeo and Juliet **24th ANNIVERSARY**

9 ARTS FILMMAKER Q&A
BY: *Mr. Watt*

Q: WHAT WAS THE *INFLUENCE* FOR THE TROMA FILM: "Tromeo and Juliet"?

Lloyd Kaufman: During a trip to Shakespeare's grave at Stratford-on-Avon, Shakespeare's spirit **entered** my body. Now, I'm not sure exactly what *orifice* **Shakespeare's** spirit **exited** my body, but it was that day; that the vision for '**Tromeo**' became clear. I had a *vision* that: what Shakespeare truly wanted when he wrote **Romeo & Juliet** was--: A *six-foot* '**monster**' & **body piercing** ---. I knew that I had to make that *dream come alive*.

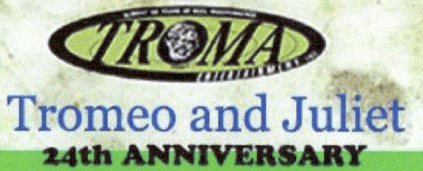

Q: WHO IS YOUR FAVORITE *MOVIEMAKER*? WHY?

Lloyd Kaufman: McG. Anyone with the **audacity** to be credited as **three letters** is alright, in my book.

Q: WHO IS YOUR LEAST FAVORITE MOVIEMAKER, Mr. KAUFMAN?

Lloyd Kaufman: Terrence Malick. His movies are overlong, pretentious sh*t.--- He needs to have a little more *McG* in him.

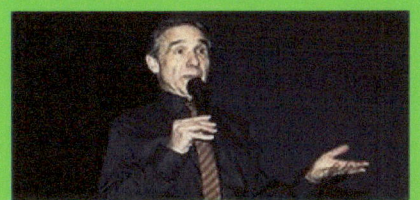

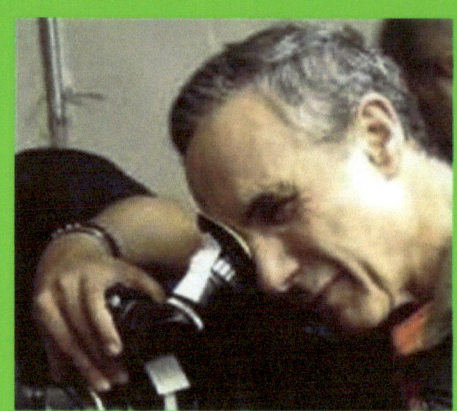

Q: WOULD YOU *RECOMMEND* ANY OTHER **MOVIES**?

Lloyd Kaufman: Attack the Block (2011) by Joe Cornish, The Sightseers (2012) by Ben Wheatley.

Q: WOULD YOU *NOT RECOMMEND* ANY OTHER MORE RECENT **MOVIES**?

Lloyd Kaufman: The Dark Knight Rises (2012). Boring, pretentious, confusing

Q: HAVE YOU HAD ANY *PLEASANT* BRUSHES WITH **STARDOM**?

Lloyd Kaufman: You're talking about something that's impossible.

Q: HAVE YOU HAD ANY *UNPLEASANT* BRUSHES WITH **STARDOM**?

Lloyd Kaufman: Yes. Cyndi Lauper *refused to sign* my copy of *Sell Your Own Damn Movie*.

Q: HOW HAS YOUR MOVIE **TROMEO & JULIET** AFFECTED YOUR LIFE?

Lloyd Kaufman: It's *extended* Troma's **40+ years** of being economically *blacklisted* by the mainstream film industry and ignored by the mainstream media.

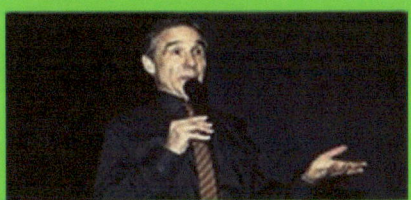

Q: WHAT ARE YOU DOING RIGHT NOW TO PROMOTE YOUR **T & J** MOVIE'S 29 YEAR ANNIVERSARY?

Lloyd Kaufman: Trying to build up the courage to get the ---- in the top right hand corner of my desk-- [AUTHOR CHOOSES TO EDIT LLOYD'S INTRESTING 'CORNER OF DESK' TALE; FOR QUIET SAKE OF **BREVITY**].

Q: WHAT IS YOUR FAVORITE MOVIE MAKING EXPERIENCE?

Lloyd Kaufman: Once again, you're talking about something that's impossible.

Q: WHAT IS YOUR LEAST FAVORITE MOVIEMAKING EXPERIENCE?

Lloyd Kaufman: Being in Israel filming *Big Gus, What's the Fuss?* (1973),

Q: ANY MOVIE-MAKER ADVICE FOR THE KIDS STARTING OUT?

Lloyd Kaufman: "To thine own self be true," a phrase coined by **William Shakespeare**, author of that best-selling book "*101 Money Making Screenplay Ideas,*" also known as 'Hamlet'.

Lloyd Kaufman's TROMEO & JULIET Movie Related Web-Links:

- Movie IMDb link: www.Troma.com/films/tromeo-and-juliet

- Lloyd Kaufman's IMDb link: imdb.me/lloydkaufman

Official Troma Entertainment Site: www.Troma.com

and he can be reached on Twitter @lloydkaufman

(PHOTOGRAPHY/ ARCHITECTURE DEPT.)

Mr. Watt's early B&W **'ARCHITECTURE, URBANSCAPES & NATURE'** photo-study series, are about dealing with evolving **societal changes**, the filmic preservation of natural scenic **loss**, & his acceptance of life's **renewal**, via **old pictures**.

His photo-studies began first, as his *own filmmaking collection* of *cinematographic images*-- then, as a monochrome statement of *'joyous expression.'*

Watt feels, that as he gets older-- his documenting & preserving the **beauty** of the **past** & **present**, helps him to deal with his own **cultural anxieties** (of "...so much **cultural change**, in so **short** a time period", he says) & also dealing with the **'Now's'** uncertain advent of *hope* and the challenges, of the unknown **future**!

One of his *fine-art* examples of this *self-therapeutic* concept, is seen in one of the upcoming *vintage-looking* photograph samples (on the next page): **"The City & The C.N. Trains.'** The Toronto, Canada based photograph, he says, was a **suboncious** pictorial study, of North America's growth; through technology & rapid travel (especially with the Canadian **C.N. Trains**, shown moving through a growing **metropolis**, of the **future**.... ever **changing** the landscape, for upcoming **generations**).

Also, The *heart-warming* shots of **'28 Lennox'** (1 & Interior 1), an old office building (just before being torn down), is an example of the **past** ---making way for the **future**... Enjoy the photos & his **photog essays**, o'Art Lovers, wherever U are!

(Mr Watt wants to also let you readers know, that the B&W **'ARCHITECTURE, URBANSCAPES & NATURE'** pictures that follows' Photo-prints are avail. on **TonyWatt.com** & Redbubble.com , as well. ~B.S.

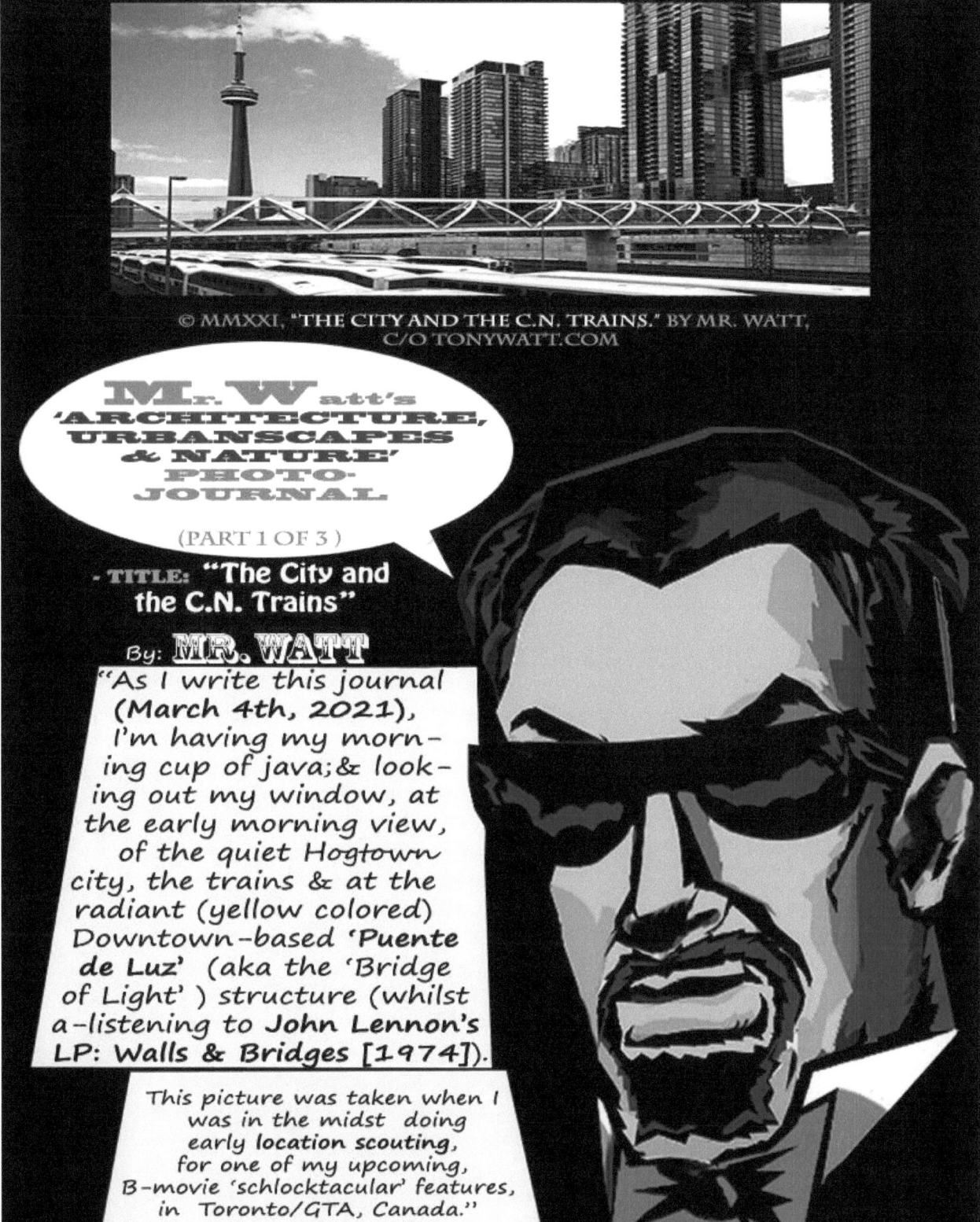

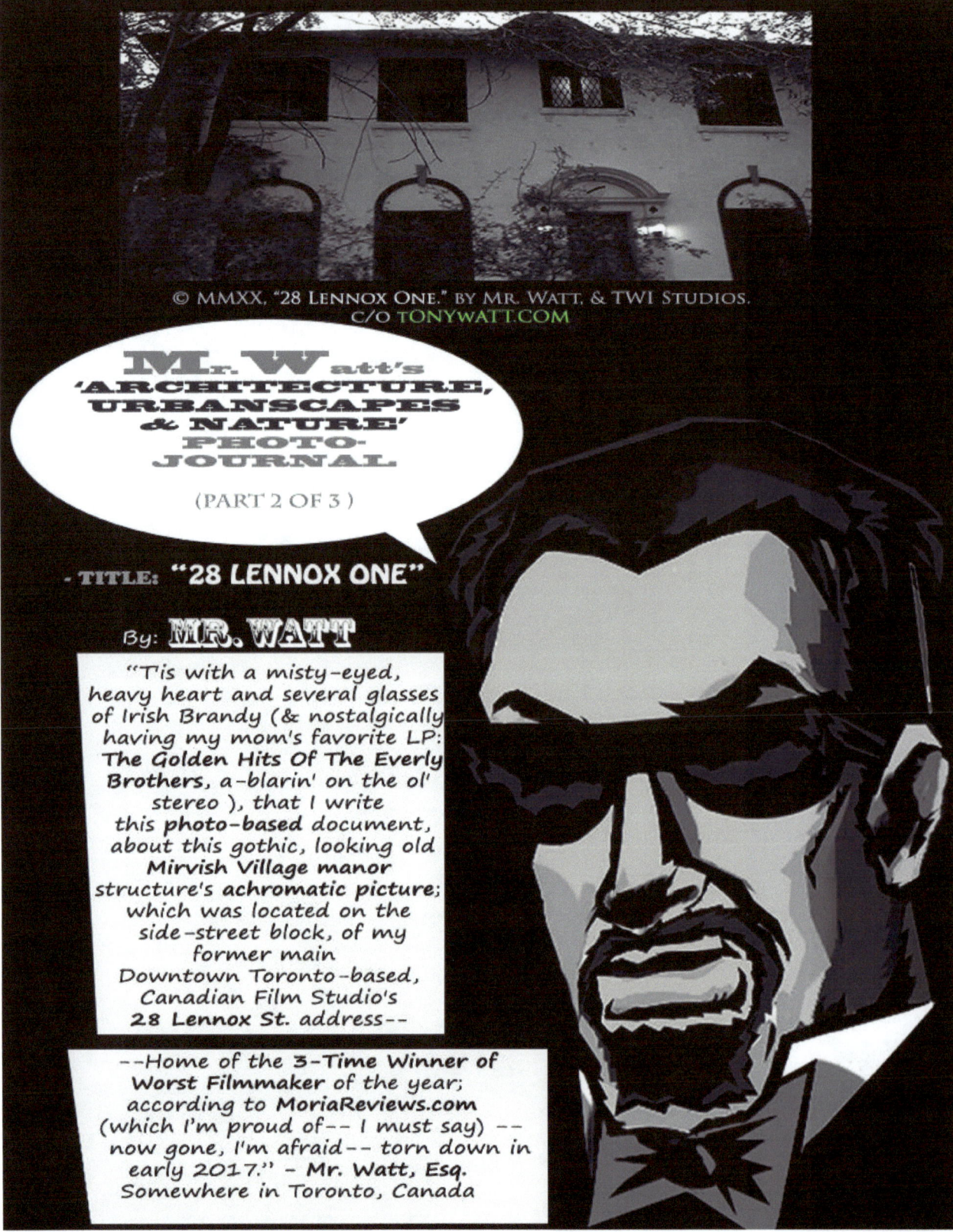

© MMXX, "28 Lennox One," by Mr. Watt, & TWI Studios.
c/o TONYWATT.COM

Mr. Watt's 'ARCHITECTURE, URBANSCAPES & NATURE' PHOTO-JOURNAL

(PART 2 OF 3)

- TITLE: "28 LENNOX ONE"

By: MR. WATT

"T'is with a misty-eyed, heavy heart and several glasses of Irish Brandy (& nostalgically having my mom's favorite LP: *The Golden Hits Of The Everly Brothers*, a-blarin' on the ol' stereo), that I write this photo-based document, about this gothic, looking old Mirvish Village manor structure's achromatic picture; which was located on the side-street block, of my former main Downtown Toronto-based, Canadian Film Studio's 28 Lennox St. address--

--Home of the 3-Time Winner of Worst Filmmaker of the year; according to MoriaReviews.com (which I'm proud of-- I must say) -- now gone, I'm afraid-- torn down in early 2017." - Mr. Watt, Esq. Somewhere in Toronto, Canada

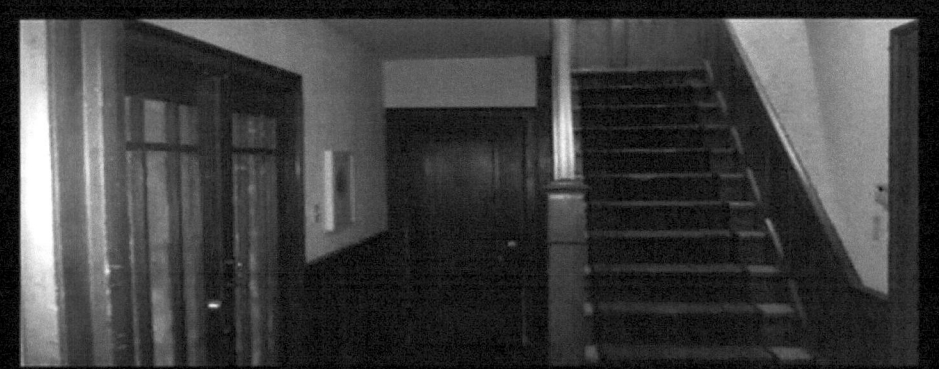

© MMXX, "28 Lennox Interior One", by Mr. Watt, & TWI Studios.

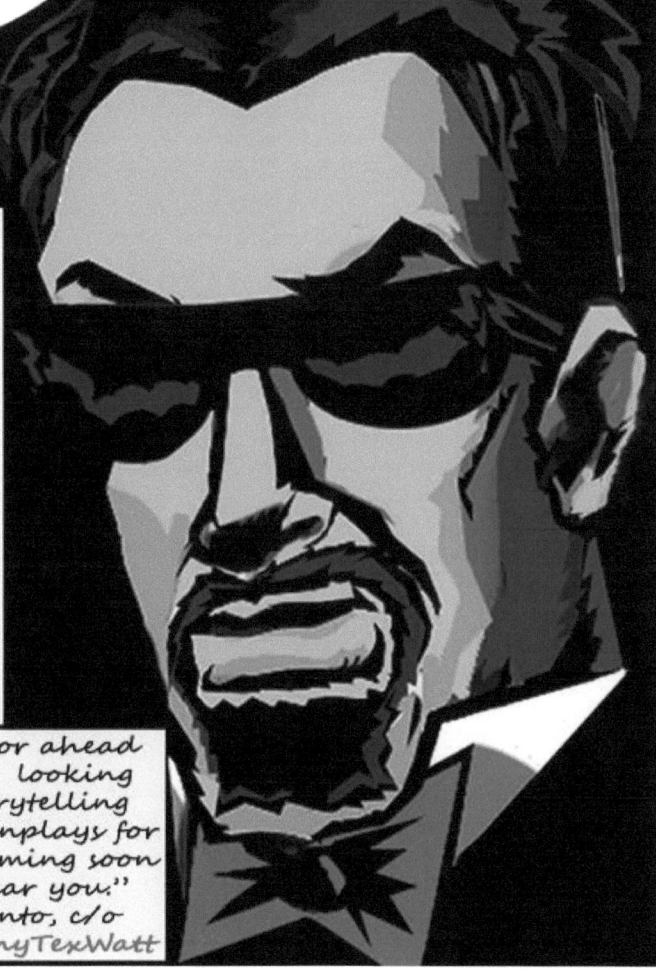

Mr. Watt's 'ARCHITECTURE, URBANSCAPES & NATURE' PHOTO-JOURNAL.

(PART 3 OF 3)

"As I write this photo-journal, I'm having my usual morning cup o' java, (and listening to Kate Bush's LP *The Kick Inside* ('78).

- TITLE: "28 LENNOX INTERIOR ONE"

By: **MR. WATT**

And, just as this Mirvish Village location's similarly named first 'exterior' shot previously-- I called this B&W 'Urban-scape' picture: '28 Lennox Interior One' (the decaying mansion-like Victorian building was sadly demolished, in Feb. '17). If one squints, you can (on either L.&R. sides) you can see the vintage push-button light switches, beside the doors (one button was for lights 'on' ..the other for 'off'...quite charming, I must say).

The foreboding, mysterious door ahead & the mysterious, foreboding looking stairway's fantasy-horror storytelling potential; influenced the screenplays for a few self-produced projects...coming soon to a cinephile watch party near you."
-Respectfully, Mr. Watt, Toronto, c/o TonyWatt.com & My Insta @ TonyTexWatt

The 9 ARTS PLAYWRIGHT Q&A

for JOHN ROSS BOWIE's Rock & Roll comedic Play: 'FOUR CHORDS & A GUN'

~ article by ~
Mr. Watt

[THEATER & LITERATURE DEPT.]
PROLOGUE

~ IMAGES c/o STARVOX ENTERTAINMENT

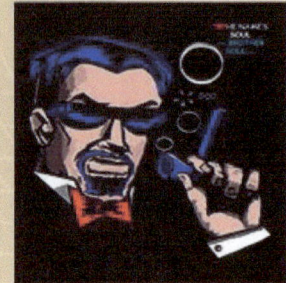
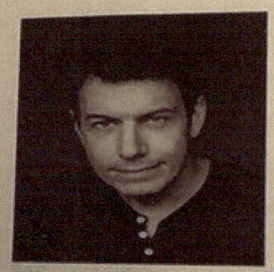
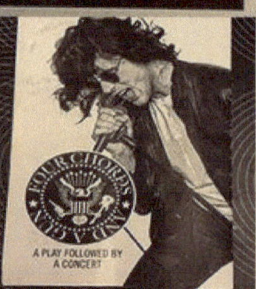

On a cool 2021, Toronto, Ontario SPRING DAY,--as he sat & listened to the *mood energizing* Ramones' Greatest Hits *album* & various 'CLASSIC ROCK' cassettes, with his old Sony Walkman headphones, blasting on *Level '11'* -- Then *accidentally* erasing this article's original 'PROLOGUE', from the P.C. screen--

--- THE AUTHOR: MR WATT, calmly 'PG' cursed-- sat back down, with immense exotic java & typed-up this last rewritten [THEATER/LITERATURE DEPT.] 'zine-article's 'Prologue' --- after having assembled his scanned original '4 CHORDS & A GUN' playbill info together, with the superb D.Katz's press-pix JPEGS (graciously sent by Starvox Entertainment's Exec. Asst. Carla ~ Re:Impresario/Producer Corey Ross' Theatrical Production approved 'photo request' for Mr. Watt's 9 Arts Magazine article), to match up with the following showcase story, for popular performer: John Ross Bowie's first written live feature play: Four Chords and a Gun (after Watt successfully completed his Hollywood-based interview, for 9 ARTS' first "Theater & Literature"-based Q&A---nicely set-up & arranged by the L.A. office, of talent rep: Steve Muller & Katie, his helpful exec. assistant, for the neo-playwright, Bowie -- who is also a successful actor [Speechless, The Big Bang Theory, Jumanji: The Next Level, Children's Hospital & The Heat]).

In said interview, John Ross Bowie chats with the author about Watt's seeing & enjoying his play, based loosely on the real-life rock icons, The Ramones (a band listed very high in Rolling Stone Magazine's Top 100 Greatest Artists who), who had worked with legendary producer/inmate Phil Spector (who had an unusual propensity towards brandishing fire-arms) and how the event led the band to destruction. The play's 2019 Toronto/Chicago production director Richard Ouzounian, said in a past interview that he knew he had to direct the play, when he first read the script. He also quoted: "...it (the Four Chords and a Gun script) told me stuff about the Ramones, that I never knew-- and, it told me stuff about Phil Spector, that I thought I knew-- but, didn't realize that it was as **bad** as it really was."

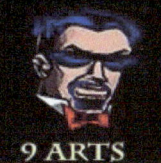

9 ARTS MAGAZINE

[THEATER & LITERATURE Dept.]

STARVOX ENTERTAINMENT'S 2019 Production of:
JOHN ROSS BOWIE'S
"FOUR CHORDS & A GUN"
(A play about PHIL SPECTOR & THE RAMONES)
A PLAYWRIGHT'S PERSPECTIVE

Actor-turned-Playwright John Ross Bowie, has a chat with the author (in the upcoming **9 ARTS** Q&A), about the feature play he wrote-- based on the infamous 40+ year old story ---

---of how the Ramones (the troubled, legendary, pioneering underground American New York City recording legends, OFTEN cited as the 'fathers of punk rock')---

STARVOX ENTERTAINMENT/COREY ROSS PRESENTS

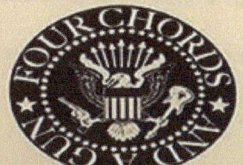

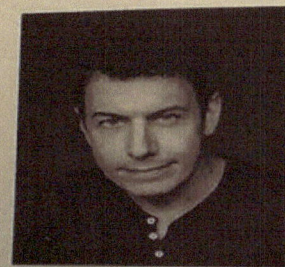

WRITTEN BY
JOHN ROSS BOWIE

WITH
JUSTIN GOODHAND CYRUS LANE RON PEDERSON
PAOLO SANTALUCIA JAMES SMITH VANESSA SMYTHE

SET & LIGHTING DESIGNER	ASSISTANT SET & LIGHTING DESIGNER	DIALECT COACH
NICK BLAIS	HANS KRAUSE	DIANE PITBLADO
COSTUME DESIGNER	GUN WRANGLER	WIG DESIGNER
MING WONG	RICHARD COMEAU	SHARON RYMAN
STAGE MANAGER	APPRENTICE STAGE MANAGER	FIGHT DIRECTOR & INTAMACY COACH
MILLY MAGUIRE	EMMA MONET	SIOBHAN RICHARDSON
SOUND DESIGNER	MUSIC DIRECTOR	PROJECTION DESIGNER
JAMES SMITH	PAUL MOODY	ALEX WILLIAMS
GENERAL MANAGER	PRODUCTION MANAGER	PRODUCTION ASSISTANT
VALERIY KOSTYUK	JEFF HERD	WENDEL WRAY
DIRECTOR, MARKETING & SPONSORSHIP	TOUR & MARKETING MANAGER	TOUR & MARKETING COORDINATOR
LESLIE-ANN DOMINY	GREG JUKES	DANIELLA RICHARDS
TICKETING MANAGER	ACCOUNTING	SOCIAL MEDIA	PRODUCER
JONATHAN HOLMES	DAVID BLYE	DALE BOYER	COREY ROSS

~ IMAGES c/o **STARVOX ENTERTAINMENT**

DIRECTED BY
RICHARD OUZOUNIAN

-- who worked with the controversial music producer Phil Spector (who had a propensity towards brandishing *fire-arms*) and how the event led the band to destruction.

[THEATER & LITERATURE Dept.]

In *April, 2019*, after the **9 ARTS** Q&A, interviewer & his movie-maker buddy, *Score*, saw a *Starvox* advert, that the Toronto live entertainment company's impresario *Corey Ross*, was bringing Bowie's popular, new **'4 CHORDS & A GUN'** U.S. 'rock' play to Canada-- This article's writer & a few music & theater supporting *drinkin' buddies*, got tickets to the Canadian *Fleck Theatre* premier, in the scenic **Toronto Harbourfront** area *(Ross, had, after enjoying the 'gutsy, funny & intriguing' script, with 'moving characters' [brought to him by his good friend Ouzounian, the Toronto director], also had mounted a Chi-Town run, as he'd stated: "What's good in Toronto, is good in Chicago.").*

Upon entering the Fleck Dance Theatre ---*Mr. Watt*, your *intrepid scribe*, enjoyed the *pre- & after-show's* near-cultish, Rocky Horror-like denim & leather-jacket based, cosplay-like *party atmosphere*--

STARVOX ENTERTAINMENT/COREY ROSS PRESENTS

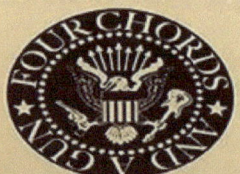

WRITTEN BY JOHN ROSS BOWIE

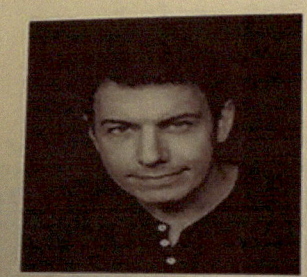

-- of a huge throng of Toronto's finest theater audience *members-in-black* (many *buzzed!* Caught up in the, wonderfully wafting *exhalation*, of totally legalized Ontarian *Reefer Madness!* ---& ghetto-blasted *Ramones* tuneage!), gathered, nattily dressed up exactly like the infamous 70's punk band (& a few cheaply perfumed, but, elegantly nutty *weirdos* in retro-disco-suits, gold-chains & bad wigs; coppin' *Phil Spector's Style* [?]...like a weird disco *Twilight Zone* episode)!

It was a lovely, culturally mixed audience, of *downtown chic* meeting the *suburbs*, for sure!

At any rate--'Gabba gabba we accept you, we accept you ,one of us' ---in the next few pages, enjoy **9 ARTS'** enlightening Q&A, interview with *Playwright*: **JOHN ROSS BOWIE!**

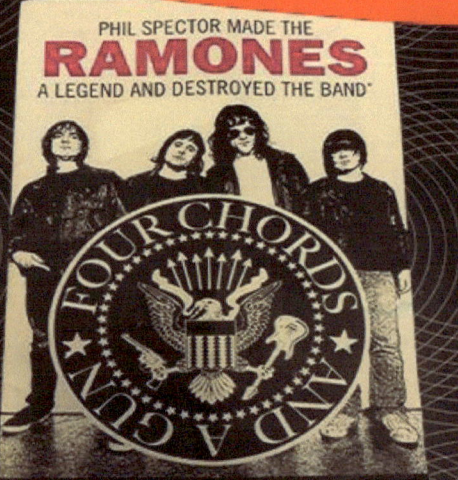

~ IMAGES c/o **STARVOX ENTERTAINMENT**

(2019 TORONTO PRODUCTION)

ACTORS

Justin Goodhand	Joey
Cyrus Lane	Johnny
Ron Pederson	Phil
Paolo Santalucia	Dee Dee
James Smith	Marky
Vanessa Smythe	Linda

9 ARTS MAGAZINE
~ IMAGES c/o STARVOX ENTERTAINMENT

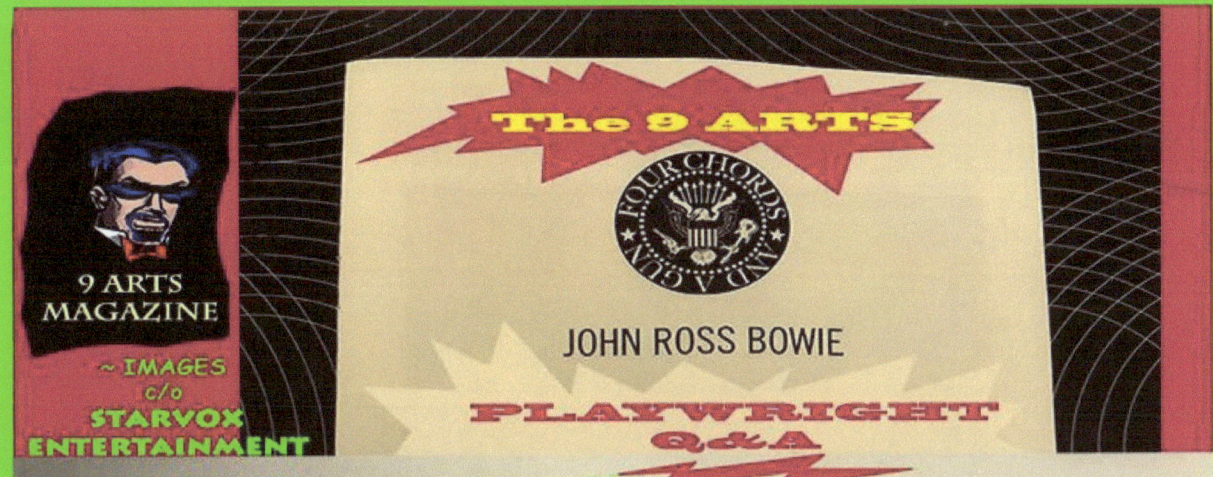

The 9 ARTS
JOHN ROSS BOWIE
PLAYWRIGHT Q&A

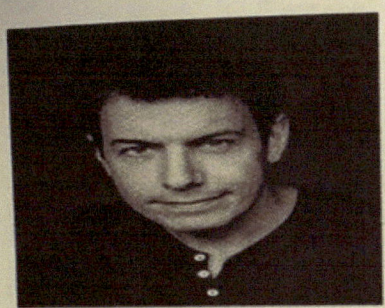

JOHN ROSS BOWIE (Writer)

John Ross Bowie is best known for his role as alpha nerd bully Barry Kripke on *The Big Bang Theory* and as dad Jimmy diMéo on *Speechless* with Minnie Driver. Bowie is also a member of the Upright Citizen's Brigade, and works quite often with The Daily Show alum Rob Cordry, including on the cult series *Children's Hospital* on which he played Dr. Max von Sydow. And he used to play bass in a punk band called *Egghead*.

BY: *Mr. Watt*

Q: So, to do a quick *summary* for our readers--- for at least, as far as what I saw of your revised version of the play -- set in the dying days of 1979, at the conflicted, violent tension-filled Phil Spector led, L.A. mansion-recording sessions, of the Ramone's *End of the Century* LP. What was your main reason for choosing this particular topic, as your first *playwriting effort?* ---the subject matter, or the characters?

John Ross Bowie: The *characters* were the main draw for me – I loved the idea of all these *disparate personalities*, with wildly *different work ethics*, coming together to make something *great*.

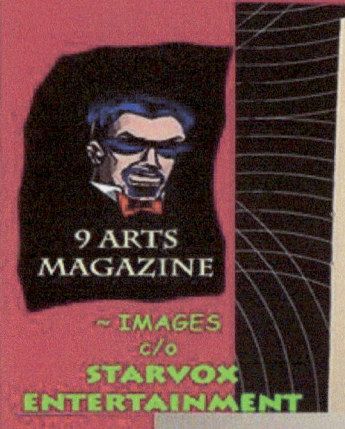

The 9 ARTS
JOHN ROSS BOWIE
PLAYWRIGHT Q&A

9 ARTS MAGAZINE
~IMAGES c/o STARVOX ENTERTAINMENT

JOHN ROSS BOWIE

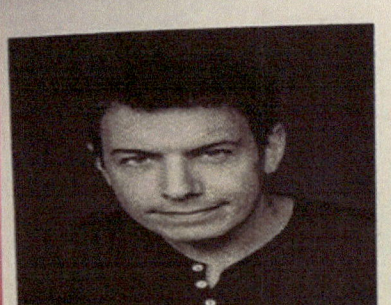

Q: The FC&AG's play poster tagline says: "Not a f***ing musical!" —why did you want to make that point clear, or, was this just a clever *marketing slogan*?

Answer: The "Not a f***ing musical" tagline came from the *producers* in Toronto, but, *I didn't mind it*. It's important that the audience get ready for what they're seeing--- which is *not a jukebox musical*, but a *kitchen sink drama* about *mental illness* & *ambition*.

Q: How did you feel, as a member in the audience, about the *overall* 2019 *Toronto* & *Chicago* crowd's after-show reaction & seeing the 6 *FC&AG* characters come to life, *LIVE*---- (*SCRIBBLINGS*) that you had *originally* wrote, as *inkspots* on a *page*?

Answer: I loved the cast from the **Toronto** and **Chicago** production, they were *really beautiful*. I do feel like the play benefits from a smaller, more *intimate space*. Those theaters were pretty big, and the play loses something when you don't feel like you're really in the *same room* with these people.

Q: How were you, in **FC&AG** ever able to *sift out, compartmentalize* & *flesh out* your written takes on the personalities, of each individual *Ramones* band-member's *characterizations* (with each of their *unique traits* ,, other than with their usual, *public guitar-slingin', lip sneering*) Taxi Driver/Saturday Night Fever-like (70s TV sitcom) 'Nu Yawker' *tropes & street accents*?

Answer: I was very careful to make sure each *character* could be *distilled* into something *playable*. Joey (Ramone) wants to *make art* that lasts, Linda (Ramone) wants to *be respected* and *heard*, Johnny wants to *be rich*, etc. The *main point* of *this play* was to take *these people*, these *flesh and blood people* who have been reduced to *cartoons* and *names on a t-shirt*, and explore what made them *real*.

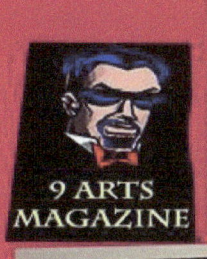

9 ARTS MAGAZINE

The 9 ARTS

JOHN ROSS BOWIE

PLAYWRIGHT Q&A

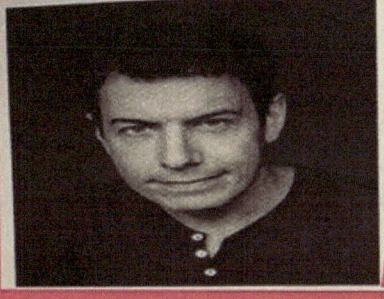

Q: Were you ever *involved* in any kind of *live theater productions* (before you wrote the play), in the past?

Answer: The *joke answer* is I became a **playwright** because I hate *money*. I've always loved going to the **theater**, since I was a *kid*. I'd like to do more theater as an *actor*, definitely. There's an *immediacy* and an *intimacy* to *theater* that you can't find *anywhere else*.

Q: How did you first *decide* to become a *playwright*?

Answer: I was having *no luck* writing **screenplays** or **pilots** that I wasn't really invested in, so I thought "*f**k it*", let me write something small, for a *smaller audience*, but that's about something I *love*.

Q: Was it your *past experience* of being involved with many cinematic *dramas, comedies & live performance projects* that helped your *writing*? And if so, how?

Answer: I think my experience as an *actor* helped my writing. I wrote with an eye towards giving everybody **stuff to do**, making sure everybody has a moment or two. Even though it's not a *musical*, it's structured little like one: **Joey** has an "*I want*" song, **Phil** has a sort of bad guy *aria* at one point. **Actors** really seem to enjoy doing the show, which is satisfying as hell.

Q: Your story skillfully combined recognizable NY urban-cool with slick, snarky L.A. showbiz smarminess tropes. A lot of the play's material seems to be written from personal experience...is it?

A: I think ultimately I'm an *east coaster* who loves being on the *west coast*.

Q: Which Coast do you most identify with *East, or West*?

A: I think I can sympathize, though, with the *Ramones* in this play. LA is weird and alienating at first, and I tried to get that sense of *confusion* across in the play. **Dee Dee** proclaims early that "most of *Beverly Hills* is flat! F***ing flat! No **Hills**! WHY AREN'T THINGS WHAT THEY SAY THEY ARE?!" That's not Dee Dee talking, that's 2002- era, *John*, having just moved to *Hollywood* and desperately trying to get his bearings.

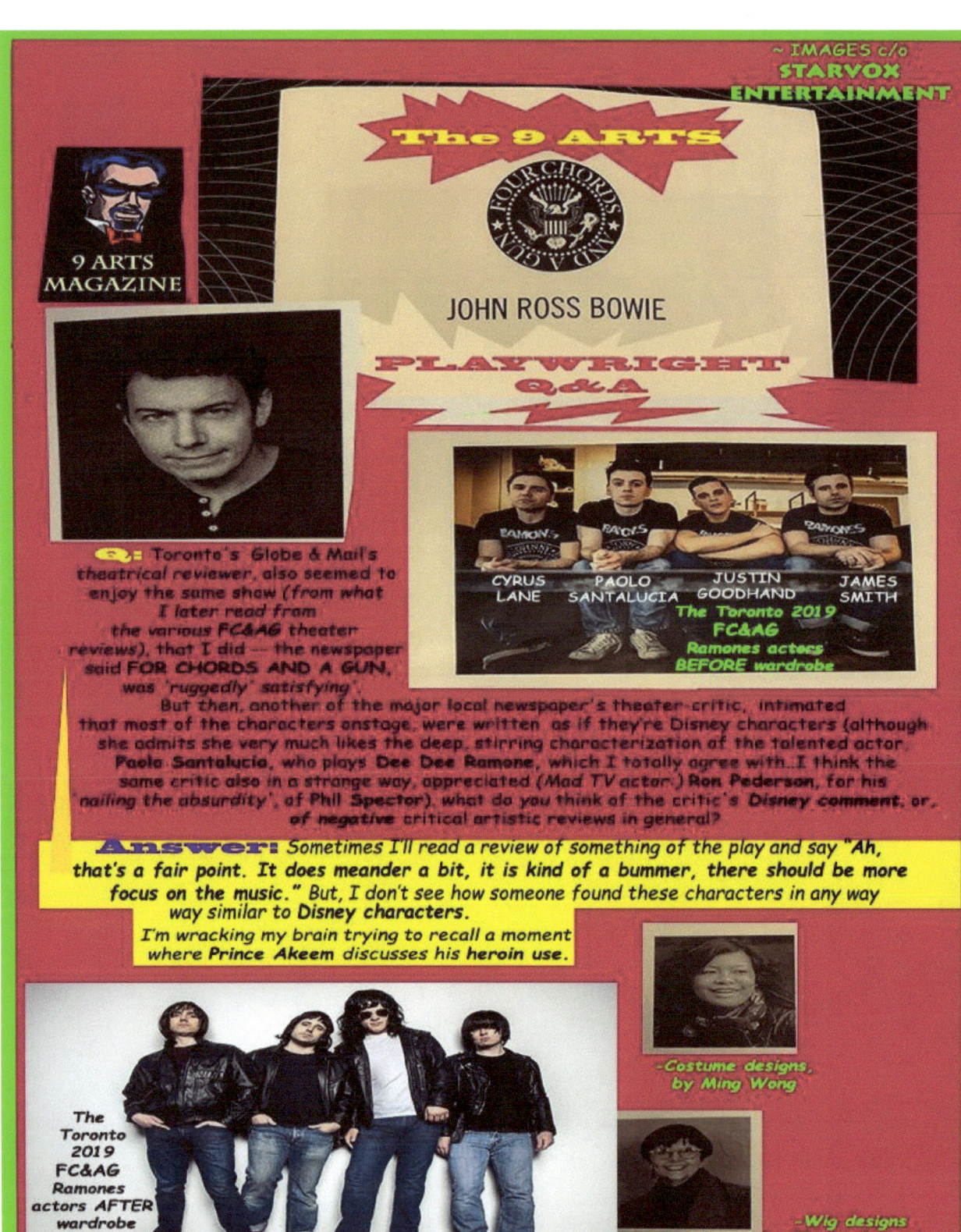

The 9 ARTS
FOUR CHORDS AND A GUN
JOHN ROSS BOWIE
PLAYWRIGHT Q&A

9 ARTS MAGAZINE

~ IMAGES c/o STARVOX ENTERTAINMENT

CYRUS LANE • PAOLO SANTALUCIA • JUSTIN GOODHAND • JAMES SMITH

The Toronto 2019 FC&AG Ramones actors BEFORE wardrobe

Q: Toronto's Globe & Mail's theatrical reviewer, also seemed to enjoy the same show (from what I later read from the various FC&AG theater reviews), that I did — the newspaper said FOR CHORDS AND A GUN, was 'ruggedly' satisfying'. But then, another of the major local newspaper's theater critic, intimated that most of the characters onstage, were written as if they're Disney characters (although she admits she very much likes the deep, stirring characterization of the talented actor, Paolo Santalucia, who plays Dee Dee Ramone, which I totally agree with. I think the same critic also in a strange way, appreciated (Mad TV actor,) Ron Pederson, for his 'nailing the absurdity', of Phil Spector), what do you think of the critic's Disney comment, or, of negative critical artistic reviews in general?

Answer: Sometimes I'll read a review of something of the play and say "Ah, that's a fair point. It does meander a bit, it is kind of a bummer, there should be more focus on the music." But, I don't see how someone found these characters in any way way similar to Disney characters.
I'm wracking my brain trying to recall a moment where Prince Akeem discusses his heroin use.

-Costume designs, by Ming Wong

-Wig designs by Sharon Ryman

The Toronto 2019 FC&AG Ramones actors AFTER wardrobe
Photo by Dahlia Katz
JOHNNY • MARKY • JOEY • DEE DEE

~ IMAGES c/o **STARVOX ENTERTAINMENT**

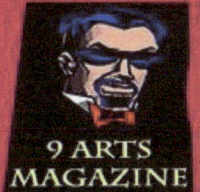
9 ARTS MAGAZINE

The 9 ARTS

JOHN ROSS BOWIE

PLAYWRIGHT Q&A

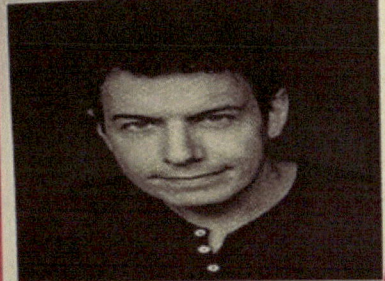

Ron Pederson *played* **PHIL SPECTOR**

Q: And, John, would you have a Hollywood casting bucket-list, for each of the 6 characters, if a FC&AG movie is ever made? (*NOTE* Not only would I heartily recommend the four band lads [Goodhand, Lane, Smith & Santalucia], as well as (Smythe) the talented actress from the 19 Toronto cast, for if a *Four Chords and a Gun* feature-movie [or TV series project is ever made, with this Canadian cast in mind]— If I had to pick a standout...my personal thumbs up 'green light', vote for casting, would be the memorable **Ron Pederson** ---He has the edgy presence of a young Al Pacino...my own vote--- if I may say--- [and I'm sure Starvox's Corey Ross would agree] he'd be a classic choice to play the cinematic version of the controversial Phil Spector]

Answer: Pedersen is great, and a good guy to boot. Honestly, I've been blown away by every cast. I would love for you to have seen **Josh Brener's** *Phil*, or **Larz Justice's** *Johnny*, or a very early version of Phil played by **Ben Feldman**. Or **Mike Cassady's** *Dee Dee!* **Arden Myrin's** *Linda!* So Good! As I said earlier, I wanted to write a play because there could be more *intimacy* in the writing AND fewer *commercial concerns*. I wasn't interested in a soup to nuts *biography*. I thought it would make more sense to just focus on this one album and all the craziness that went into it.

Q: FC&AG is set in Los Angeles with mostly street-flavored N.Y characters, masterfully directed by the Canadian (former Toronto Star Theatre Critic & former Theatrical Stratford Festival Assoc. Director) **Richard Ouzounian**, ---How did Toronto impresario/producer **Corey Ross'** Starvox Entertainment Touring Company get involved with **FOUR CHORDS & A GUN**?

Answer: Richard Ouzonian ---(the)--Canadian director heard about it and flew himself down to **Tulsa** to see a production of the show. We had lunch and he was so *enthusiastic* about the project and what I was trying to do that he wanted to take it up to **Canada** and find a producer. So the *director* came before the (the FC&AG play's) producer.

[IT IS HERE, THAT I MUST NOTE, AS A 2ND ED. DRAFT ADDENDUM, THAT IN MY FURTHER CHATS WITH THE PROD'CR **MR. COREY ROSS** IS, HE'D TOLD ME THAT HE HAD FIRST FOUND THAT THE INTRIGUING CHARACTERS IN THE PLAY'S EARLY SCRIPT WERE VERY INTERESTING & MOVING, WITH IS WHY HE CHOSE TO TOUR **4C&AG** IN THE **US & CANADA** ~ W.)

~ IMAGES c/o **STARVOX ENTERTAINMENT**

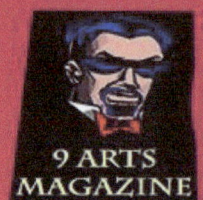
9 ARTS MAGAZINE

The 9 ARTS
FOUR CHORDS AND A GUN
JOHN ROSS BOWIE
PLAYWRIGHT Q&A

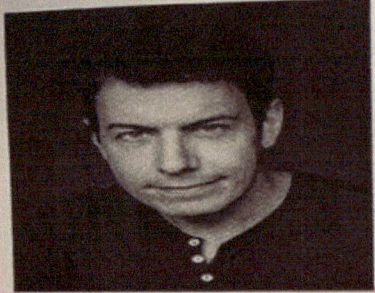

Q: What influenced you to do a revised script for the *2019 FC&AG Toronto/Chicago Production?* And also, what is the *difference between this 2019 play*, that I saw in *Toronto, Canada* & the version that had it's debut in *L.A.*.?

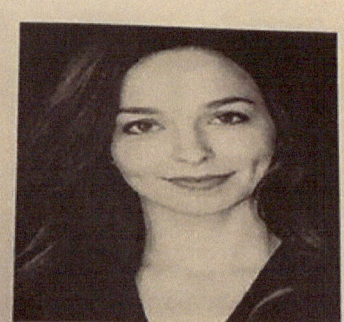

Vanessa Smythe *played* **LINDA RAMONE**

Answer: The big difference is **Linda** (**Ramone**'s presence in the play, portrayed by actress: **Vanessa Smythe**) -- with every draft her character gets more agency. I think this is *faithful* to the *real person*; in every interview it's clear that Johnny fell in love with her because she took no sh** and *gave as good as she got*. So I try to honor that by *dimensionalizing* her character a bit more with every *revision*.

Q: Nice. I've also heard somewhere, John, that the director, Mr. Ouzounian strongly suggested that the 2019 Toronto Starvox Entertainment Production's script draft should increase the sole 4C&AG Play's female character Linda (as portrayed by Smythe the talented & very moving Toronto Actress/Writer) & more scenes with her were added. Why was that done, Sir?

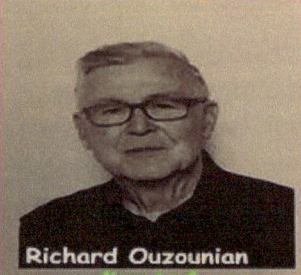

Richard Ouzounian *directed* **FOUR CHORDS & A GUN**'s 2019 Toronto/Chicago Production's Theatrical run

Answer: *SPOILERS FORTHCOMING*: He asked for one more scene after the big confrontation, a scene that shows **Joey** and **Linda**, after they break up. [writer edits next few words Hitch-cockian Style for the selfish act of protecting another 4C&AG Play's [Spector] Character's critically controversial dramatic **opus**).

~ IMAGE c/o **STARVOX ENTERTAINMENT**

~IMAGES c/o **STARVOX ENTERTAINMENT**

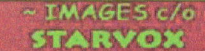

9 ARTS MAGAZINE

The 9 ARTS

JOHN ROSS BOWIE

PLAYWRIGHT Q&A

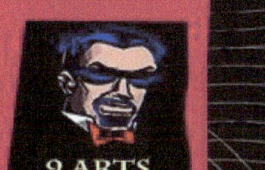

Q: I and my closer theatrical audience associates (see: drinking buddies) really enjoyed (besides the rockin' closing band) the play's edgy acting & the realistic, theatrical retro-flavored mood & feeling of Nick Blais' vintage stage production & lighting designs-- & the '70s costumes & wig designs......as well as your and Richard Ouzounian's choice of soundtrack music throughout the play's performance-- Who's decision was it to have a LIVE band performance, after the play? And why?

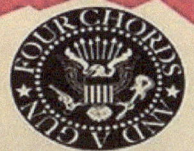

NICK BLAIS
Set & Lighting Designed
FOUR CHORDS & A GUN's
2019
Toronto/Chicago
Production's Theatrical run

Answer: Starvox, the producer (Corey Ross) based out of Toronto thought it was a fun way to close out the show and remind the audience why the band was so fun.

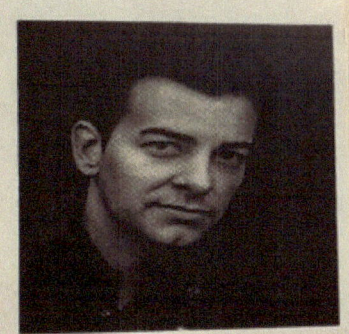

COREY ROSS
Produced
FOUR CHORDS & A GUN's
2019
Toronto/Chicago
Production's Theatrical run

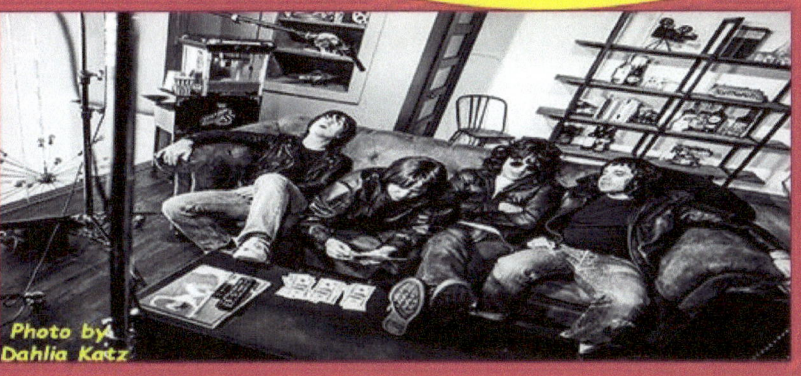
Photo by Dahlia Katz

~ IMAGES c/o
STARVOX ENTERTAINMENT

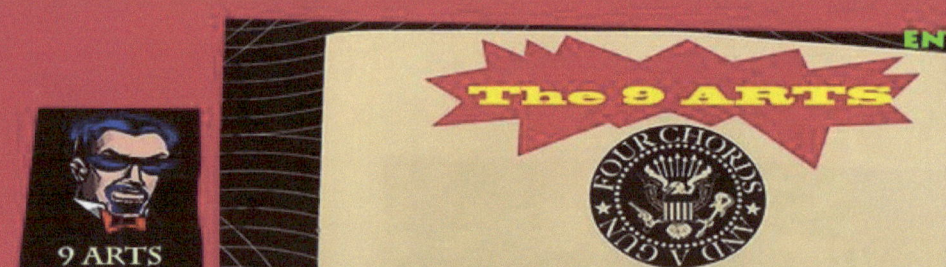

9 ARTS MAGAZINE

The 9 ARTS

JOHN ROSS BOWIE

PLAYWRIGHT Q&A

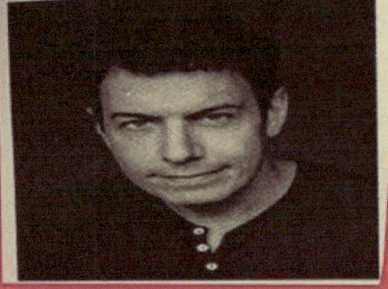

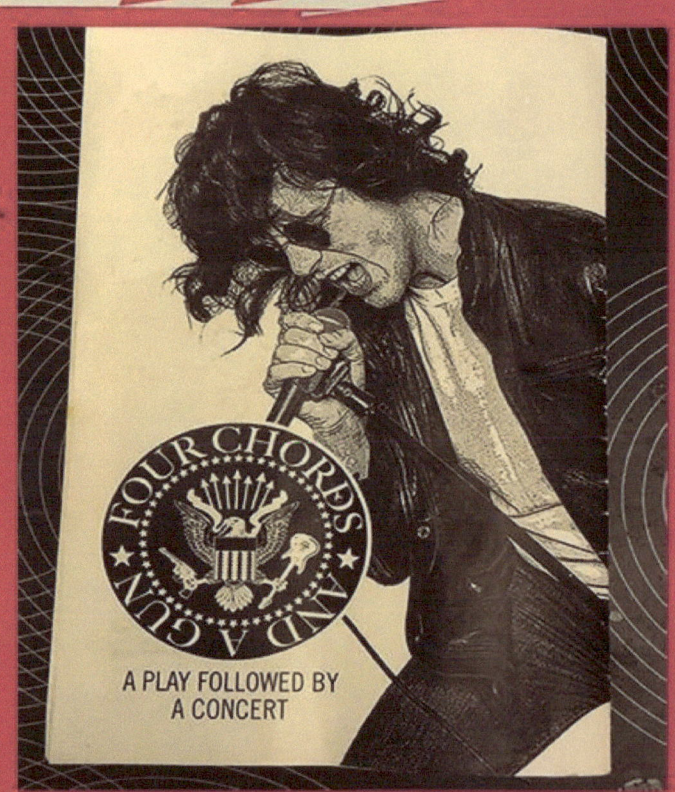

A PLAY FOLLOWED BY A CONCERT

Q: Do you have any favorite *playwrights, or screenwriters*? If so, what were their *influences* on your written *work*?

Answer: I really like **Tony Kushner's** writing – he's not against having his characters just *stop* and *hash* through ideas. He's also *really funny*. He's not above putting a critique of the *modern left* right next to a d**k joke, and I find that endearing. **Angels in America** is amazing, obviously, but a **Bright Room Called Day** and **Homebody/Kabul** are also smart and moving. I love **Tom Stoppard** and I love **Peter Shaffer** – **Amadeus** was, believe it or not, a big *inspiration* to me, while I was writing my play.

Q: Cool. In retrospect--- in your full reflection of *FC&AG*, today, 2021-- after all is said & done--- how has the past *combined* 2019 theatrical *critiques* and *audience reaction* about *FC&AG's* scripted storytelling & stage shows, affected your *view* of the *revised* '19 theatrical production, moving forward? Will you react, to the dramatic critics & do another script revision, for future productions, or, are you *happy* where the written play *stands*?

Answer: This is a good *follow up* question – enough reviews bemoaned the lack of Ramones music --that I went back & looked at the script, and found an *organic way* to insert it (the songs played *between the scenes* are in the script, and are there for specific reasons). There's a *new scene* – not yet staged – where **Phil** puts on '*Sedated*' and picks apart why it's such a great *pop song*. I hope it sees the light of day.

~IMAGES c/o **STARVOX ENTERTAINMENT**

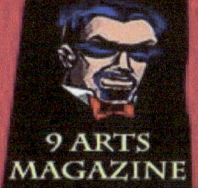

The 9 ARTS

JOHN ROSS BOWIE

PLAYWRIGHT Q&A

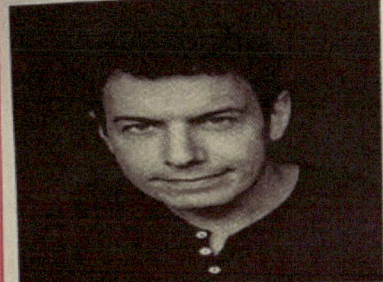

Q: Did you find it *easy* to juggle the story's humor vs darkness, black vs white, hard rock vs pop-panache, within the play's 90 minute story, for dramatic/black comedy *entertainment purposes*?

Also, John, how were you able to orchestrate your *storytelling*... do you write for *yourself*, or your *audience*?

Answer: I write with *myself* in mind first, but I'm not trying to *alienate* an audience. I try to *alternate* between the *shattering moments* of *real life* and the silly, *dumb moments* of real life. Some *hysterically funny* things happened right around the time my mom *passed*, in 2018 – life is like that.

I tried to bring those *contrasts* into the play. Not just the ones you mentioned, but the *dichotomy* between right and left politics, *inspiration and practice*, spontaneity and rigidity. I think the play is firing nicely when those contrasts are being presented with a certain amount of *balance*.

Q: I assume that with your various talents, that you can you see the final multi-media results (Like the FC&AG characters, the whole costuming, the eerie vintage atmosphere, period designs & costuming) projecting like a 70s B- movie, in your mind's eye (as you were writing & structuring & the play, during pre-production.)--
---Were you?
Or, was everything a satisfying *surprise* during *post-production* & the final *stage performances*? Were there any scenes in the 2019 Toronto/Chicago stage run, that blew your own mind?

Answer: It's interesting – I try to go easy on *stage directions* because I want a *director* to enjoy *staging it*, to feel like they have some *independence* in *approaching* the *material*. If I wanted to *completely control* every aspect of the look and feel of the story-- I'd write a *novel*.
So there were some *lovely surprises*, yes – *a swinging light* here, a surprise use of *projections* there. A production in *Oklahoma* had Phil *pop out* of a *road-case*, that had been sitting down *stage left*, for the first *15 minutes* of the play. I gasped but it was wonderful.

~ IMAGES c/o **STARVOX ENTERTAINMENT**

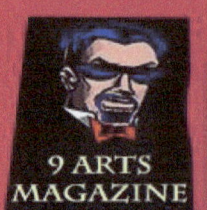
9 ARTS MAGAZINE

The 9 ARTS
JOHN ROSS BOWIE
PLAYWRIGHT Q&A

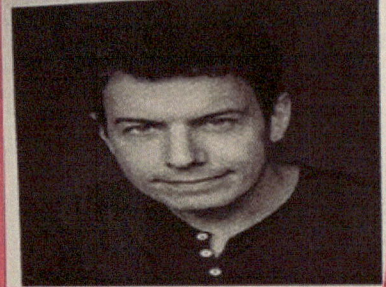

~ IMAGES c/o **STARVOX ENTERTAINMENT**

Q: Was FC&AG ever ever validated by any The Ramones members, or Phil Spector?

Answer: A couple people who worked for the *Ramones* saw it and liked it. I did an interview with *Monte Melnick*, the Ramones' *tour manager*, who was initially quite hostile to the very idea of the play. But the more we talked, and the more he saw that I was a huge fan who had done a ton of research, the more he warmed up. I'd love for him to see it at some point.

Q: Thank you for the interview, Mr. Bowie, now in closing-- have you got any other advice for upcoming playwrights?

Answer: A) the worst *vice*, is advice --but also **B)** --find out who you are in the play, who's your proxy, and find out what your *proxy* wants. If you can't find anyone in the play who represents you even *a little*, maybe this isn't your play to *write*.
For me, it was *Joey*. I understood Joey's *romanticism* and his *endless creativity*, his need to *belong* and his need to make something that *lasts*. I mean, why else would a *marginally* successful TV actor *suddenly write a play?*

John Ross Bowie's FOUR CHORDS AND A GUN THEATRICAL Related Web-Links:

PLAYWRIGHT's IMDb WEBSITE: *imdb.me/johnrossbowie*

- PLAY'S 2019 TORONTO PRODUCER Website:
starvoxent.com/

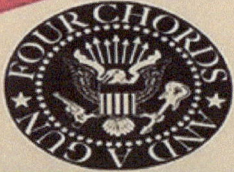

- PLAY Website:
4ChordsPlay.com

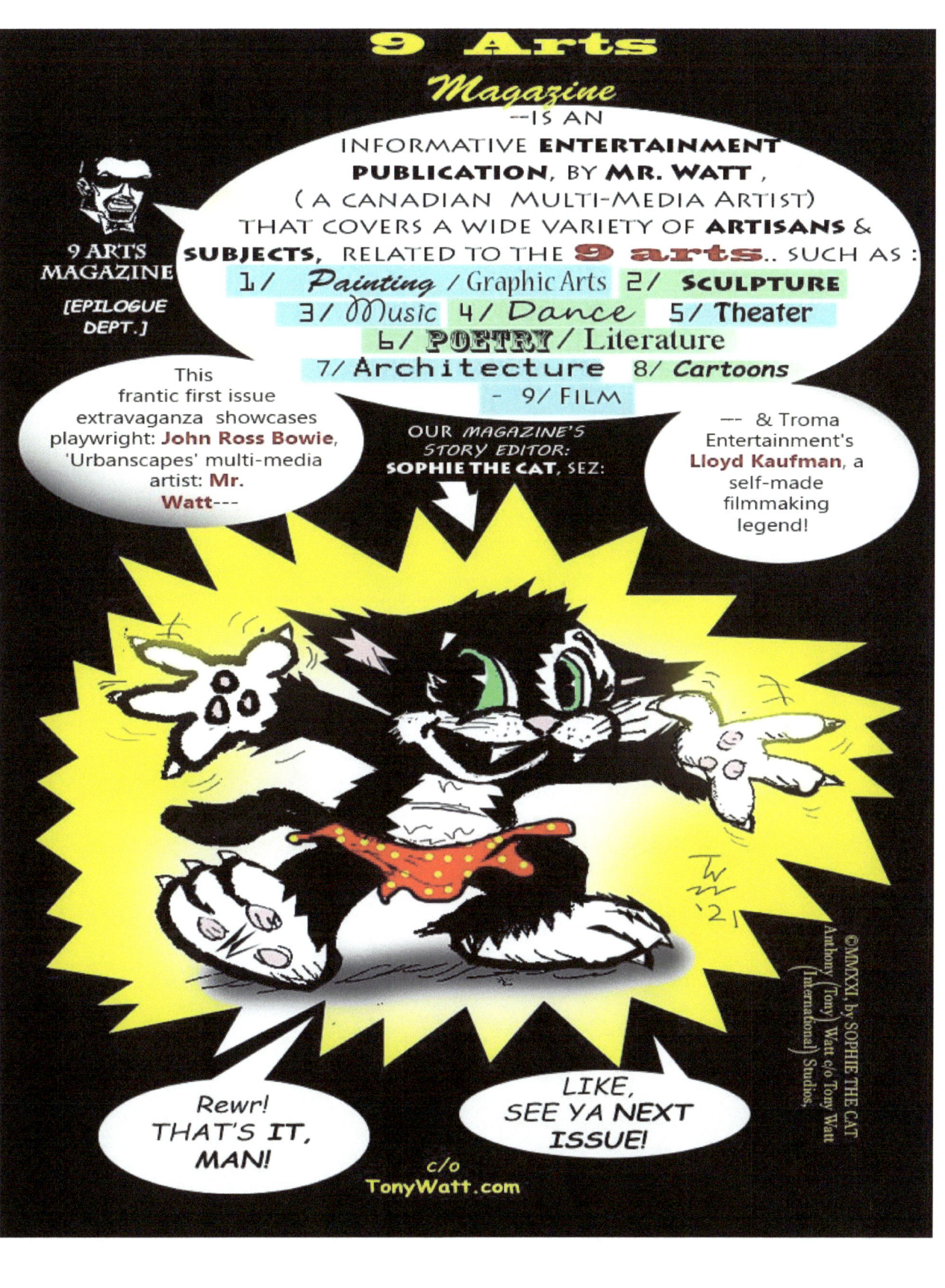

www.ingramcontent.com/pod-product-compliance
Lightning Source LLC
Chambersburg PA
CBHW040408220526
45473CB00004B/1174